NEW QUALIFIED TEACHERS

AND OTHER ENTRANTS INTO TEACHING

ESSAYS IN LEADERSHIP FOR CHANGING TIMES

Edited by

Judith Fenn and Nigel Richardson

Published for the Independent Schools Council Teacher Induction Panel and the Headmasters' and Headmistresses' Conference by John Catt Educational Ltd

2009

First Published 2009

by John Catt Educational Ltd,
12 Deben Mill Business Centre, Old Maltings Approach,
Melton, Woodbridge, Suffolk IP12 1BL
Tel: 01394 389850 Fax: 01394 386893
Email: enquiries@johncatt.co.uk
Website: www.johncatt.com

ISBN: 978 1 904 724 735

Set and designed by
John Catt Educational Limited

Printed and bound in Great Britain
by Bell & Bain, Glasgow, Scotland

CONTENTS

About the Contributors

John Baugh was born in Uganda and educated at Aldenham School and St Luke's, Exeter. He played professional football before deciding to do a proper job, and previously taught at Haileybury before becoming Headmaster of Solefield School, Sevenoaks (1987-1997), Edge Grove School, Hertfordshire (1997-2002) and the Dragon School, Oxford (2002-) which is the UK's largest boarding and day preparatory school, with 850 pupils. He was chairman of the Boarding Schools' Association in 2007.

Chris Brown read English at Cambridge, undertook his teaching practice at Marlborough, and subsequently taught at The Leys and Pangbourne before moving to Radley. Having been head of English and director of studies, he became Head of Norwich School (1984-2002). He chaired the HMC Inspection Steering Group, was a member of the original ISI committee, and was a qualified Reporting Inspector for HMC and then for ISI. He was chairman of HMC in 2001. He now acts as an educational consultant appraising Heads and senior staff, as well as helping governing bodies in the selection of Heads.

Peter de Voil was Headmaster of The English College in Prague from 2004 until 2009, having previously been Headmaster of Frensham Heights for 11 years. He taught first at Wrekin College and then at Uppingham, where he became a housemaster. He taught for one year at Milton Academy in the USA as a Fulbright exchange teacher, and for many summers directed residential English language courses for the Bell Educational Trust in Cambridge. He has also been chairman of the HMC Community Service Committee and of HMC Projects in Central and Eastern Europe, an ISI inspector and deputy chairman of the English-Speaking Union of the Czech Republic, as well as a governor of the Treloar School for the Disabled. He is a governor of St Christopher School, Letchworth, and a member of the Academic Board of the Bell Educational Trust.

Dr Brenda Despontin is Principal of the British School in Brussels, and was previously Headmistress of Haberdashers' Monmouth School for Girls from 1997 to 2008. She has a first degree in psychology; a Master's degree on Thomas Hardy; a doctorate in children's literature; and an MBA on international leadership. After teaching at the British School in Brussels and working as a residential supervisor in a home for disturbed teenage girls, she went on to teach at comprehensive and independent schools before setting up the girls' division at The King's School in Macclesfield for five years from 1992. She was president of GSA in 2006.

Judith Fenn graduated with a degree in history from Cambridge University, after being educated in the state sector. She completed a PGCE at Thames Polytechnic, and then taught for 14 years in the independent sector, beginning her career at South Hampstead High School where she worked for nine years, latterly as senior teacher. She was appointed head of history at Sevenoaks School in 2000, and deputy head at The Godolphin and Latymer School in 2002. She joined the Independent Schools Council in 2005 with a remit to develop teacher induction and recruitment. In September 2008, she became head of Schools' Services, with additional responsibilities for the Information and Advice Service.

Nick Fraser taught French and German at the Edinburgh Academy before moving to Stewart's Melville College to become head of French. Thereafter he was head of modern languages at Hutchesons' Grammar School in Glasgow, during which time he also worked as an examiner for French within the Scottish examination system and served as a member of the group created to advise on the content and function of the online Modern Foreign Languages Environment (MFLE). He has also reviewed the content of digital material in modern languages for Learning and Teaching Scotland. He has been academic deputy at Magdalen College School, Oxford, since 2006.

Steffan Griffiths was born to a teaching family: his grandfather was the Headmaster of a primary school in Hertfordshire for 27 years; his father taught at Whitgift School for 37 years, with roles including head of department and professional tutor; and his mother was the Headmistress of Fonthill Lodge Preparatory School in East Grinstead for 18 years. After attending Whitgift himself and doing a gap-year at Timbertop, the Year 9 outdoors campus of Geelong Grammar School, he studied classics at University College, Oxford. He started teaching classics at Tonbridge School in 1995 before moving to join the classics department at Eton College in 1999. Steffan returned to Oxford in 2006 to become Usher at Magdalen College School.

Rachel Gudgeon studied at the University of York where she graduated with a BA Honours in linguistics and education before moving on to obtain a PGCE from the University of Hull's Scarborough School of Education. She specialised in early years and gained experience in primary schools in North Yorkshire. After qualifying in 2007 she took the position of reception class teacher at Terrington Hall Preparatory School, an independent school set in the beautiful Howardian Hills in rural North Yorkshire. During this time she became the early years foundation stage co-ordinator, moving the early years classes forward through the development of the early years foundation stage curriculum.

The Rt Revd Peter Hullah has been Principal of Northampton Academy since 2005, having been Area Bishop of Ramsbury (1999-2005) and Headmaster of Chetham's School of Music (1992-9). His earlier teaching posts included being assistant chaplain of St Edward's School, Oxford (1974-7), chaplain and housemaster of the International Centre at Sevenoaks (1977-87) and senior chaplain at the King's School, Canterbury (1987-92). He has also been chairman of the Chaplains' Conference (1987-92) and of the Bloxham Project (2000-6) and a governor of Marlborough College (2000-8). He is currently a trustee of Uppingham School.

Lucy Leakey graduated in 1996 from the University of Wales in Cardiff, with an honours degree in art with Qualified Teacher Status. She began her career in the state sector working as the art co-ordinator at St John's Primary School in Huntingdon. From there she became the art and, latterly, English co-ordinator at Sacred Heart RC School, in Peterborough.

In 1999, she was selected by Cambridgeshire LEA to work as a Leading Literacy Specialist within a variety of schools in the county. In 2001 she completed her MA in education through the Open University. She then worked for five years at Laxton Preparatory School and is presently an assistant head at Wellingborough Preparatory School, Northamptonshire.

Louise Moelwyn-Hughes read classics at Magdalene College, Cambridge, and took up her first post at Marlborough College where she taught classics and Arabic. While at Marlborough, where she was a housemistress, she studied Arabic at the School of Oriental and African Studies (SOAS), completed the Cambridge Certificate in Arabic and Middle Eastern Studies and received a Master's degree in education management (OU). She is currently the senior deputy head at The Perse School, Cambridge, where she has particular responsibility for pupils.

Paul Nials attained his PGCE from York University in 1980 and his MA(Ed) from Southampton University in 1998. He has worked in three independent day and boarding schools. Appointed to Portsmouth Grammar School in 1987, he has held a number of posts including head of house, officer in the CCF, rugby coach, head of PSHE, induction tutor for NQTs and, most recently, senior teacher. He acts as a professional mentor for three university PGCE courses and was appointed as a visiting fellow at Southampton University in 2003, where he serves on the School of Education Secondary Steering Group and teaches on the secondary science PGCE course.

Michael Punt graduated in 1992 from St Peter's College, Oxford, with a physics degree and then gained an MSc from Imperial College, London, in 1993. Having vowed that he would never teach, he spent eight happy years in the physics department at St Dunstan's College, south-east London, including time as a head of year, before becoming head of physics. In 2001 he moved to The Perse School, Cambridge, where he was head of sixth form and subsequently deputy head (academic). In 2007 he became Headmaster of Chigwell School.

Dr Nigel Richardson was Head of The Perse School, Cambridge, from 1994 to 2008, having been second master at Uppingham, Head of the

Dragon School, Oxford, and deputy head of the King's School in Macclesfield. He is an appraiser of Heads and teachers, a governor of several HMC schools, and was editor of the HMC magazine *Conference & Common Room* from 1999 to 2002. He has written history books for children and training literature for the Industrial Society, and contributes regularly to the educational press. He was chairman of HMC in 2007, and is currently working on a biography of the great Victorian Headmaster Edward Thring.

Amanda Triccas studied history at Westfield College, University of London, and also completed a Master's degree in European labour history at the Institute of Historical Research. Her postgraduate research into 19th century England was curtailed by her appointment to teach at Whitgift School in 1992. Five years later she joined the staff of St Paul's Girls' School and was appointed onto the senior management team as assistant deputy head in 2005. Amongst her responsibilities are staff training and induction, academic ICT and educational visits.

Tom Wheare taught history at Eton and Shrewsbury before becoming Headmaster of Bryanston in 1983. He was treasurer of HMC from 1993 to 1998 and chairman of HMC in 2000. Since retiring in 2005, he has edited the HMC house magazine, *Conference & Common Room*. He is a trustee of the Girls' Day School Trust (GDST) and a member of the executive board of the Association of Governing Bodies of Independent Schools (AGBIS). He has been a governor of ten schools and is still a governor at the Dragon School, Port Regis and Exeter School.

Introduction

Judith Fenn

Welcome to teaching. Welcome also to the independent sector. We hope this book will provide you with information about the world you are soon to enter, and insight from those already there. Teaching is both a profession and a vocation, and it often becomes a way of life. Those who work within it regularly rate their job satisfaction more highly than those who work in other professions.

Its rewards and joys are many, and there is always the knowledge that what you are doing will make a difference. The Teacher Training Agency's incredibly successful advertising campaign in 1998 'Everyone remembers a good teacher' even featured Tony Blair citing his former Headmaster, Eric Anderson of Fettes and Eton fame, while TV dramas *Hope and Glory* and *Waterloo Road* draw in the viewers and the recruits.

In recent years, higher salaries and opportunities to develop practice through further and more sustained training, regular appraisals, and career moves have gone a long way to making teaching more professional across the maintained and the independent sectors. In Chapter 14, Paul Nials, a proponent of continuing (although he may prefer continuous) professional development looks at the opportunities to develop within your first role, while Chris Brown's discussion of school appraisal systems and their benefits considers the importance of evaluating your own performance within the context of your own school.

Your first year will see you join a fresh cohort of Newly Qualified Teachers to complete your induction year, overseen by the independent sector's appropriate body, ISCtip.[1] Rachel Gudgeon and Steffan Griffiths, two former NQTs (the raw recruit from a preparatory school, and the experienced teacher from a senior school), review their very different experiences and draw key lessons from them in Chapter 2. A glimpse into the role of the induction tutor, who is likely to play a vital role in your support and development, is offered by Lucy Leakey, assistant head at Wellingborough School, in chapter 10.

The first year involves the careful planning and time management of your teaching load. 'Master time and you master your life', advises my co-editor, Nigel Richardson, in his chapter, and you may also find the sage advice offered by Nick Fraser on classroom survival, and Peter Hullah on achievement for all, to be of practical use. However, life in the independent sector is not simply about the teaching. In fact, for those of you who come to the sector for the first time, the sheer variety of schools, curricula and co-curricular activities on offer can rather boggle the mind. Chapter 1 offers an introduction to all things independent, while Brenda Despontin advises enthusiasm tempered with pragmatism towards all that is on offer beyond the classroom.

Beyond teaching colleagues there are the many wonderful support staff that enable the school to function, and there are the parents. It is a wise NQT who realises the worth of the school caretakers and kitchen staff; the bursary staff and the teaching assistants. John Baugh surveys the varied roles in a school, while Peter de Voil offers his own introduction to the independent school parent, and Michael Punt looks at the sometimes tricky issues of selection and admissions.

Finally, the legal and regulatory aspects of schools and teaching are considered by Amanda Triccas and Louise Moelwyn-Hughes. Know these and you will be prepared for the unexpected eventualities which always arise when teaching children.

Many of the broad issues dealt with in this book are fascinatingly complex. They can vary in detail, with no magic answers or one single solution fitting all; as a result, they can require fine judgements from those seeking to address them. In this series we encourage our contributors to be free-range: to write about aspects of their work without too much prescription or constraint. Occasionally you will find issues on which they see things from slightly different perspectives, although at the editorial stage we aim to filter out any directly contradictory advice.

You will find much support and excellent advice amongst your new colleagues. Do not be afraid to ask for help when it is needed. Other teachers will have been there before you, and they will be more than happy to steer you through the first year, and to celebrate your successes as you go. The years I spent in the classroom were some of the happiest and most satisfying of my working life, and I hope that they will be for you as well.

Reference

[1]The Independent Schools Council Teacher Induction Panel.

Chapter 1

Working in the independent sector

Judith Fenn

The independent sector is a strange beast: its schools often lumped together as one and called 'private' or 'fee paying', they are often labelled as 'posh' or 'smart' in the media and they are used conveniently as examples of privilege and wealth. Yet these perceptions are misleading. Schools which fall into the independent category vary enormously in size, type, wealth, and ethos. There is no such thing as a typical independent school and the distinctive feature of the sector is its very lack of homogeneity. Independent schools are exactly that – independent. While this may mean that writing a chapter of a book trying to outline what it is like to work in the sector poses some problems, it also means that the sheer amount of choice and variety available to teachers working within it is one of its unique strengths.

Independent schools are both small and large; they are day schools, and boarding schools, or a mixture of both. They are single sex, co-educational, boys with some girls and girls with some boys (usually at the top or bottom end of the age range, and thus in the prep school, or in the sixth form).

They contain a mix of nationalities and religions which provide a welcome international and multi-ethnic perspective to education and, because of this, they promote an understanding of, and a tolerance for, other points of view. So, for example, teaching modern history to a sixth form set comprising Chinese, Japanese, Lithuanian, Dutch, Iranian, English and Scottish students brings a syllabus into far sharper focus, especially when you are told by one of them: "You teach Mao as history, but for us, this is how we live."

Some independent schools cross key stage phases, catering for seven to 13 year-olds in preparatory schools, where subject specialisms are valued and the step from Key Stage 2 to 3 is seen as a natural and seamless progression. Some schools cater for the highly able, and are academically selective; others educate children of mixed ability, or cater for those with specific special needs. Independent schools are rural and urban. The rolling acres of a boarding school in Somerset seem at face value to have little in common with a small prep school in East London, or an urban day school in Manchester, yet beneath the choice and diversity offered by the sector lies a set of shared goals and values.

The sector values its teachers enormously, and recognises them as the life-blood of schools, whatever the size and type. It is committed to their training and welfare, and each year it inducts some 1100 Newly Qualified Teachers (NQTs), via its own validating appropriate body, the Independent Schools Council Teacher Induction Panel (ISCtip), which is the single largest provider of statutory induction in England[1] and which fulfils for its schools the role of a local education authority. Every NQT in an independent school knows (s)he is part of a cohort of teachers which will be supported, trained, and assessed against a set of nationally recognised standards. The induction year experience is rated highly by the NQTs, with more than three quarters of them valuing the support given to them by their induction tutors and mentors.[2]

The framework in which new teachers operate is designed to support and encourage them within the individual context of the school. The NQT year has a rhythm of its own which complements the academic year, whilst encouraging reflection and the charting of progress. The mandatory 10% timetable reduction gives a breathing space in a busy schedule. Regular lesson observations and meetings provide opportunities to celebrate successes, to plan for future events, and to diagnose weaknesses via carefully selected targets. Half-termly and termly formative reviews measure progress against the core standards (which build on those attained during initial teacher training), and these standards reflect accurately what a teacher should be doing in his or her daily job in their first years in post. They engender good practice, and encourage constructive criticism. The summative assessments (three over the course of the induction period) combine to confer fully-qualified status on NQTs and the induction year is validated by the General Teaching Council.

The ISCtip NQT profile[3] suggests most are PGCE trained (some 70%); more fall into the 25 to 29 age group; some have completed the Graduate Training Programme (GTP) (17%); and some 13% are already experienced teachers. It is noteworthy that the award of Qualified Teacher Status (QTS) is not mandatory in the sector, so many prefer to embark on training. They include some who are senior figures in their school.

The sector looks after its teachers by providing an environment conducive to pupil learning. The low pupil:teacher ratio gives its schools smaller class sizes and allows the teachers to teach, rather than spending time fire-fighting disruptive behaviour. These two inter-related factors are the most frequently cited reasons for working in an independent school. A small note of caution ought to be sounded here: this is not to say that a new teacher should expect a class of angelic children whose perfect behaviour is matched only by their perfect grades. Children are children wherever they may be, and the subversive, bored, bright child in the back row on a warm Friday afternoon is a particular independent school challenge for the NQT – but more of challenges anon.

The sector values the whole child and his or her education. This should mean that curricula are inventive and flexible, pastoral care is excellent, and co-curricular activities are many and varied. Independence of teaching means that the sector looks long and hard at the whole range of qualifications and syllabi that are available, and chooses the most suitable.

The national press spends much of the post examination publication period gleefully trumpeting the growing ease of examinations, the dumbing down of traditional subjects, and the increased take-up of 'soft' options. Independent schools can choose what is best for them, and for their pupils. The majority do still follow the traditional GCSE and A level syllabi, but they do it thoughtfully, not slavishly, and a growing minority are both considering and adopting alternatives.

The International GCSE, the International Baccalaureate (both the Diploma and the Middle Years Programme) and the Pre-U have all had thousands of newspaper column inches devoted to them recently. Of course, no single curriculum is The-Answer-to-The-Problem-of-'what-to-teach-to-young-people-to-ensure-they-are-suitably-stretched-and-developed-intellectually'. Often, therefore, alternatives run happily side-by-side with traditional courses, allowing maximum flexibility and choice, and allowing teachers to deliver a carefully directed syllabus to those who are best suited to it.

The opportunity to teach a completely different curriculum is a professional development opportunity that is virtually second to none for secondary teachers. Even with the recent syllabus changes at GCSE and A level, it is so very easy to slide into an annual rhythm of delivery and results (via re-sits), but a new curriculum brings a new ethos and provides intellectual stimulation and often a much needed review of pedagogic practice.

The value the sector places on the whole child is not simply about what is taught and how it is learned. The pastoral support systems put in place to nurture and support learning are rightly praised by school inspectors, and valued by the children who experience them. House staff in boarding schools take on a duty of care far beyond their colleagues in day schools, yet the problems and issues faced by both are similar.

Being a child or an adolescent in the early 21st century is a complicated affair. Peer pressure and bullying, the lure of the internet, eating disorders, and the twin demons of sex and drugs keep tutors occupied, perhaps as much with relevant and necessary training and preparation as with the actual reality of the problems. Despite the impression sometimes given in the media, a plague of any or all of these does not appear to be infecting all schools in the country.

Beyond the confines of the syllabus and the classroom, independent schools provide a breadth of experience second to none. The opportunity to participate in the wider life of the school, and hence in the wider world, is the third most popular reason, after class size and behavioural issues, for teaching in the sector.[4] This stems from the fact that the independent school day is an extended one. Whether this is in a day prep or secondary school, or a 24/7 boarding school, the list of clubs, activities, initiatives, speakers, events, and visits is long and varied.

Teachers choosing to work in the sector rightly participate in these activities, and schools rightly place due emphasis upon them. Lunchtimes and after-school clubs are the norm; evening visits to theatres are frequent; weekend fixtures fairly common (as indeed is the Saturday morning school phenomenon in some schools although these days mostly only in those which have boarders).

Overseas expeditions push back the boundaries of education. The recent visit by boys at one major boarding school to Rwanda, to learn more about the genocide and the country's moves towards reconciling victim and perpetrator, whilst aiding in a reconstruction project, will have a long-term impact on every participant. At the same time the Outward Bound course for eight year-olds on a wet Welsh weekend will also play its part in the development of the whole child.

Independent schools are inveterate raisers of money for charity, whether at home or abroad. Sponsorships of projects, often small and less well-known or fashionable, provide opportunities for creative fundraising. Teachers may well steer and facilitate (something which they also do for pupils taking part in the excellent Young Enterprise scheme) but they know that by encouraging independent thought and initiative they are doing far more than enabling charitable giving.

Independent schools foster local links because they see themselves as part of the community, and they know that facility sharing for a joint state-independent school production or running classics lessons for local residents is all part of the broader educational experience (which is that education is always a two-way street).

For some teachers, the level of sporting achievement and the expertise and facilities that enable it, are key factors in deciding where to teach. Former independent school pupils feature in the Premiership and Football League (all 17 of them),[5] in the national teams for the Rugby Union World Cup (eight members of the 2003 World Cup winning side), battling for the Ashes in cricket, and contributing variously and vigorously to Team GB in the 2008 Olympics.[6]

Choice and opportunity attract new teachers into the independent sector, but once there, what can they expect? The rewards of teaching are great, but so too are the challenges. It is not a profession for the fainthearted, perhaps because it is half-profession and half-vocation. The first year can be unbelievably tough and tiring, and there will be times when the cycle of preparation, planning, delivery, reflection and marking seems unending and unremitting.

Yet the emotional lows of the first year are more than matched by the highs. Yes, the emotional carapace necessary for any teacher's survival is not yet fully formed, and hence NQTs are more vulnerable than their more experienced colleagues; but the joy of delivering a successful lesson, of forging a relationship with a class over time, and of seeing the results of efforts made, produce a euphoria which more than sweeps all the negatives away.

Of course it helps to be prepared for the good and the bad, and it helps to have a realistic view of the school of choice, and of the sector in which it sits. If one chooses to teach in a school which is fully boarding, because the facilities are sublime, the holidays are long and accommodation is offered, one should not be surprised by the weekend and evening duties, the need to drive a minibus, and Saturday morning lessons.

An NQT choosing a small school because of its emphasis on the personal, because the Head knows every pupil by name and because he or she is hands-on, will realise quickly that it is not only is the Head who is distinctively hands on, but so too are all the staff, with responsibilities and chores widely shared. Choose the independent sector if you are happy *not* to leave at 3.30 or 4pm because you are running a debating club, or organising a life class. Expect parents to be interested, keen (and in some cases over-keen), and informed. Expect them sometimes to be assertive: to question if not your judgement, then your comments, or your choices.

Above all, know that there are six hurdles to overcome in the first year: (i) the lack of time; (ii) endemic tiredness; (iii) a steep learning curve; (iv) unhelpfully placed pressure points in the academic year; (v) germs; and (vi) the need to admit weakness and to be honest both with and about you.

The year will pass incredibly quickly. In fact, it will gallop by. The first week blurs into the autumn term; blink, and the carol service will be upon you. Days are full, evenings equally full with preparation. Be organised – and by this I mean a military-operation-the-like-of-which-has-never-been-seen-before kind of organised. Write lists: you may not cross a lot of items off them in any one day, but at least you'll know they exist. Plan ahead where possible. Identify deadlines in advance (see iv above). You will feel tired. Don't make many hard and fast plans for your first autumn half-term break unless they include the possibility of having to catch up on some sleep and recharge your batteries. November can be the longest month and by Christmas you will feel ready for a proper holiday.

Tiredness is a common occurrence for all the best teachers, and you need to ensure you do not fall into the habit of planning and preparing 'til the wee small hours. Avoid at all costs pulling an all-nighter, because while this may have worked at university when a deadline loomed, at university the lure of the return to bed as a just reward for endeavour always existed. It's not an option for an NQT.

At school, the lure of the lively Year 7s/Upper Thirds/first years (another foible of the sector: teach in six different schools and there will be six different ways of labelling year groups) hardly offers an equivalent reward. Being new to the school means you have a lot to learn in a short time (unless you completed a GTP there, or you are an experienced teacher undertaking an NQT year, in which case the expectations of you in Year 2, or even Year 22, will be raised accordingly).

Visiting your new school prior to the onset of term, reading the staff handbook, and referring to it regularly (rather than asking someone, or guessing its contents) will ensure you are familiar with the policies, practices and procedures in the school. Knowledge is power (and it saves time) – use it. Be aware that at the times of term you feel most tired, you are also likely to have additional administration, such as grades, exams and reports. Plan these carefully and learn to juggle marking demands with a report writing week.

As a new staff member, you will be new to the germ pool of the school. School bugs come in waves (the end of September first cold; the cold+ of the late autumn; the two-days-into-the-Christmas-holiday-cold-and-cough, and the bronchial cough in February), and while you will be lucky to escape unscathed, you will fare better if you look after yourself, get enough sleep, and invest in Vicks First Defence or a suitable alternative brand equivalent.

Finally, accept that you cannot attain perfection in your teaching in Year 1: there will be good and bad days, and you will need to reflect constructively on weaknesses with the help of a mentor, colleague or head of department, and to learn from them. Accept constructive criticism from experienced colleagues: they know the subject, the school, and the children far better than you, and they are actually on your side and want to help you progress.

Realistic expectations and planning for the hurdles to be jumped will go a long way towards maximising the many benefits and rewards of teaching in the sector. The tangible ones of class size, behaviour, and access to first class facilities, have already been discussed and these go together with good pay levels and favourable conditions. However just as important is a reward which in some ways is less tangible: job satisfaction. This is far harder to quantify because each person is different, as is each job, in each school.

Teachers make an impact on those they teach and satisfaction comes from making that impact a positive one: instilling a love of a subject or topic; encouraging scholarship; engendering curiosity and the ability not to take things at face value. However, if the independent sector really does educate the whole child, job satisfaction is not simply about subject or key stage based achievement. Perhaps the greatest pleasure comes in the cyclical nature of the life of a school, as children join, grow and develop academically, behaviourally, socially, and then move on to be replaced by a new cohort.

Following a child's progress over five or seven years, following a class and its changing dynamics over two or three years, produces its own rewards. The unruly Year 9 pupil who becomes the most dynamic member of the upper sixth; the poacher-turned-gamekeeper; and the underachiever who suddenly hits his or her stride add depth and colour to a teacher's sense of satisfaction.

If something is hard, and if something takes time, the rewards seem that much more tangible and lasting. Teaching in the independent sector is not an easy or soft option, and the challenges which exist take time and effort to overcome, but once conquered the job (or vocation, or profession) is the most rewarding that anyone is likely to have. Having it also happens to be a privilege.

References

[1] It also inducts NQTs in Wales.
[2] ISCtip NQT survey, 2009, B Galeotti on behalf of ISCtip.
[3] ISCtip NQT survey, 2007, as above.
[4] ISCtip NQT survey, as above.
[5] ISC blog, October 2008, Rudolf Eliott Lockhart.
[6] The 2004 Olympics where research by The Times found that upwards of 45% of British medal winners attended an independent school.

Chapter 2

First impressions

Rachel Gudgeon and Steffan Griffiths

Each year, the independent sector welcomes NQTs fresh out of training and university, as well as mature entrants, career changers, and those with teaching experience who have decided to obtain Qualified Teacher Status as a way of furthering their own continuing professional development. In this chapter, we look at two very different NQTs' experiences of their induction year.

From a new entrant
Rachel Gudgeon

Why did I choose to work in an independent school? Before my application for the position I had worked as a tutor for children, some of whom attended local state schools and some independent schools. I was taken with their relative maturity, and knowledge of the world. The independently-educated children I worked with were polite and conscientious, had a lovely sense of fun and humour and were always ready for the next challenge. Through my positive and negative experiences whilst teaching in local state schools during my PGCE year, along with the small class sizes and extra opportunities on offer in the private sector, I decided that I would like to apply to teach in an independent school.

At interview I remembered the advice I had been given: lots of handshakes and big smiles and these were greeted throughout the day with lots of handshakes and smiles in return, welcoming me but still retaining the formality of the interview process. I was met by the school secretary at the impressive front entrance and then interviewed in the Headmaster's study by the Head and deputy head. I was, of course, nervous being at my first interview and didn't really know what to expect, but I was reassured and put at ease by the friendly approach and warm reception on arrival.

Before my interview I spent a good deal of time studying the application pack sent out to me, as well as the school website, through which I gained a good first impression of the school's ethos and the family atmosphere I was to expect. The pack and website revealed the great extracurricular opportunities, such as the outdoor education programme (including climbing and kayaking) and the pastoral care system (which involved, amongst other things, the provision of evening activities for the boarders), available for me to get involved in at the school.

Following the interview with the Head I was taken to look around the department I would be working in: the pre-prep. Here I had the chance to meet the team and to spend time with the children. Although I was not asked to teach a lesson, I did have a chance to interact with the children at play. This time during my interview day was highly valuable to me as I was able to see how happy and bright the children were.

I sat outside and read a story to some children who were looking at the books, and had the chance to ask them questions in this informal situation. The smart school uniforms, the busy activity of the children and, of course, their huge smiles really welcomed me to the pre-prep and I could already imagine myself teaching them in the classroom that would be mine. Being able to spend some time with the children really made a lasting impression on me. I will always remember how inquisitive and enthusiastic they were.

I was also introduced to my future teaching assistant and given the opportunity to ask her some questions: how long had she worked there? How many children were expected in the class next year? Was she looking forward to the summer holidays? She was very open and honest. We were able to talk about work and about our home lives. It soon became obvious that we shared a similar sense of humour. Altogether, these experiences on my interview day gave me a very positive impression of the team I would be working with.

I accepted the team's invitation to stay for lunch and I learned a great deal by taking part in this key element of the school's daily routine. The traditional way the children were seated at lunchtime, served their meal by their teacher at the head of the table, and given seconds of pudding, were all very impressive. After lunch I had a final interview with the head of pre-prep in which she reviewed my application details and asked more questions. She then gave me a smile, shook my hand and said that she would like to offer me the job!

Having been appointed as the reception class teacher all I had left to do was to complete my PGCE, spend the summer recovering from the intensive year of teacher training and excitedly prepare for my first teaching job and first class in September. The head of pre-prep was very helpful in giving me keys to get into the school and into my classroom over the summer and in handing over information about my class. She welcomed me with lots of helpful advice. My teaching assistant was keen to meet up at the school during the summer holidays. We spent time preparing the classroom together, creating our teaching space and sharing ideas. This time together put us both at ease and built our relationship before term started.

Before term started in September all members of staff were asked to attend a meeting to run through the school calendar for the coming weeks, to discuss changes that may have been made and to introduce the new members of the team. Afterwards we went to the village pub where I had the chance to meet the other teachers and staff and we were bought lunch – which of course gave me another good impression!

During my first week as an NQT everyone was finding their feet: children, parents and me. I was very open with the parents, telling them that I was newly qualified and that this was my first job. All were very understanding and warm towards me. The first morning at school was very exciting and I knew that for some parents it would be quite an emotional experience as many were sending their children to school for the first time. Having activities already planned brought the children straight into the classroom and gave me time for introductions to the parents. It also ensured that there were not too many tears.

Along the way, I've learned a great deal. During the first term the pre-prep team nurtured me and helped whenever I needed it. My teaching assistant was invaluable in her help and advice; she knew the routines and the resources available and brought many great ideas to help teaching through topics.

Asking for help and advice showed that I was willing to follow her lead and that I valued and appreciated her contributions. It can often be seen as defeatist to ask for help, and I have seen NQTs who have made their lives very difficult by trying to do everything on their own. Accept help where it is offered. Show what you are trying to achieve and how it can be done, and lead practice by working together and taking on the ideas of those you work with.

What of the NQT induction process? During my first week I was able to meet the mentor who was to support me through my NQT year. We planned regular future meetings and observations and put into action my reduced timetable allowance for that year. It was helpful that my mentor had previously taught the reception class, so she was able to offer practical advice as well as help to set targets and make observations.

During my NQT year I was able to visit early years departments in other local independent schools. This was a useful experience as I was able to compare practice in teaching and learning, and I picked up some great ideas for delivering literacy and numeracy sessions. I attended the regional NQT training sessions each term and was able to meet other NQTs working in independent schools. The training sessions had some good guest speakers and workshops, but most of all they offered a valuable opportunity to make friends who were going through the same experiences.

At my weekly meetings with my mentor we discussed the Professional Teaching Standards[1] and worked through them, finding evidence and ways of collecting evidence to meet the standards. I was able to identify areas of practice that I wanted to improve upon, and my mentor gave suggestions of local authority courses I was able to attend such as Health and Safety and Child Protection, as well as age-specific courses on phonics and letters and sounds.

Reflecting on it all at the end of my NQT year, I felt an enormous sense of achievement. I was extremely proud of the progress my class had made and, having been welcomed and nurtured during my first year of teaching, I too felt warmth and belonging towards the department and the school as a whole. I had begun that first year with apprehension and excitement, and felt that my progress through it had prepared me well for my following year, and on into my teaching career.

Without openness and honesty shared, without problems overcome, and without the acceptance of help and advice, I would not have felt so emotional at the end of term. My little class was ready to move on and up, as I was ready to start again with my new class, confident with the knowledge and experience I had gained during my NQT year.

Reference
1. TDA Professional Teaching Standards, 2007

From someone already established in the profession
Steffan Griffiths

My path to QTS is an unusual one. Despite coming from a family of teachers, and as a student half-heartedly resisting an inevitable draw to the profession, after graduating in 1995 as a classicist from University College, Oxford, I started teaching immediately at Tonbridge School before moving after four years to Eton College.

There was no statutory need for me in the independent sector to qualify as a teacher; indeed, when I started, there was a perception in both schools that a PGCE was neutral or negative in its effect. So why bother? And if I was going to bother, why wait until 2004/5 to enrol in the Graduate Teacher Programme? Moreover, by April 2009 I was Usher (deputy head) of Magdalen College School, Oxford – hardly the most obvious career stage from which to consolidate QTS. How did it all come about?

Despite the help in my first post of a very able and supportive head of department, I confess to having started with the somewhat cavalier attitude that teaching was based merely on knowing one lesson's worth more than your charges and having enough charisma to keep the 'orrible lot quiet. However, once in the classroom it became increasingly clear that there was a bit more to it, and I was competitive enough to want to do things better. I became more interested in the subtleties of classroom craft and more disciplined in my professional standards, especially when I went to Eton. There, the conglomeration of talent among both boys and staff makes the classroom both a stretching and exciting place to be and the common room an interesting forum for sharing ideas.

I was keen to be serious about what was emerging as my long-term career and thus felt a general desire for a qualification to put my money where my mouth increasingly was. Partly, this was an honourable interest in good practice, but it was also candid self-preservation to 'future-proof' myself against the vagaries of financial or political upheavals in the 30 or so years of my working life to come.

I was also conscious of my good fortune in teaching at two excellent schools and of the fact that my experience of teaching might be somewhat unrepresentative of the profession as a whole; I suppose I was sensitive to the ivory-towers-Eton-classicist cliché. However, there was no real incentive for me to stop teaching to get a qualification and I did not wish to commit between 18 months and two years to a part-time PGCE, especially as, with well over five years of experience by now, I felt that the learner plates were definitely off. The introduction of the GTP scheme was thus a welcome fast-track for people in my situation and the fact that Slough Grammar School had set itself up as a centre to offer the qualification enabled me to take the plunge.

The QTS standards have changed since I took the qualification, but I remember well the gradual lifting of the jargon fog and a dissipation of the frustration that the standards continually wanted evidence of mere common sense. I recall my growing confidence in using terminology and my realisation that the standards sensibly promote reflection of things which work and processes which are important.

But most of all I remember the visits to other schools: to a tough comprehensive in Chalvey where I saw the admirable patience of the teachers in dealing with things which were on occasions heart-warming and at other times alarming; and the extended teaching placement at

Slough Grammar School with its powerful confirmation of young people's vitality and teachers' humanity interacting with them.

I acquired QTS in the autumn term of 2005 and was intending to complete the NQT year in 2006/7. However, I applied for the post of Usher at MCS and was fortunate to be appointed at the end of that term. I did not fancy the extra administration involved with having to transfer mid-year between schools and did not think having weekly mentor meetings would be the most appropriate way to start in my new role.

Thus the hiatus until Easter 2008. However, it was always unfinished business as I retained the determination to finish things off after all the work involved in filling the standards folders. So I became an NQT in my 13th year of teaching and 18 months into my deputy headship. What difference did it make to my job and what, if anything, did I learn?

In practical terms, the light-touch paperwork compared to the GTP year meant that it was not too onerous an addition. I received permission to waive the 10% reduction in teaching load; remission for my other responsibilities is substantial and I felt it was important not to reduce my classroom profile. I was also fortunate to have the assistance of a professional tutor as a mentor, who was sensitive to the fact that the fire-fighting aspects of my role would inevitably mean that some flexibility would be required.

In respect of the five themes of the induction year,[1] like many NQTs I have continued to find helpful the enforced discipline to be reflective about classroom practice and to develop subject knowledge. I still feel that my main role is as a teacher, and that getting things going well in the classroom enables me to tackle other aspects of the job with greater confidence. In terms of differences between the responsibilities of deputy head and those of a 'normal' teacher, I feel my development has been enhanced in many areas, though issues regarding classroom craft have inevitably been affected by my reduced teaching load.

The theme of developing professional and constructive relationships plays to the strengths of the deputy head's role. I am responsible for the day-to-day running of the school, so having good professional relationships with different constituencies of the MCS community is at the heart of what I do; I have approximately 15 weekly meetings with colleagues, several less frequent committees to attend or chair, and numerous one-off meetings, both scheduled and of the 'have you got a moment?' variety.

I have therefore had plenty of opportunity to learn about getting on with people with different roles in my present school. Much time is spent in liaising with heads of year and other staff over the welfare and progress of pupils, if necessary interviewing pupils on disciplinary or pastoral matters and involving their parents in the process. It also involves discussion with pupils, teaching staff and support staff to ensure the smooth running of significant school events from open mornings and examinations to primary school liaison mornings and arts festivals.

Working within the law and frameworks has also come directly under the remit of my particular responsibilities. I have had the opportunity to check and write school policies, to deal with outside agencies in the occasional emergency, and to liaise regularly with heads of section, SENCO and the safeguarding children officer over the welfare of vulnerable pupils, aspects which also touch upon aspects of theme 3, promoting children and young peoples' development and wellbeing. Perhaps the most valuable part of learning about operations of a school, which might not be immediately apparent to a classroom teacher, has been attending governing body meetings and their various sub-committees.

Relating my NQT year to themes 3 and 4 (*ie* pedagogic practice and professional skills) has not been easy because they are specifically concerned with classroom practice and I have not been in that environment as much as most teachers. Moreover, it is sometimes tricky as deputy head to get candid feedback on performance which makes theme 5 (developing practice) somewhat challenging. In other areas, of course, such feedback is all too readily given! However, even with these themes, being deputy head has thrown interesting light onto them.

Two examples: first, the regular lesson observations have been a welcome reminder of the added *frisson* introduced by the presence of an extra adult in the classroom, since I now do a good deal of lesson observation as part of the interview process for prospective staff at my own school; when lessons do not run quite as the candidates plan, I am more acutely aware that sometimes I am the reason.

Secondly, we have adopted a management information system called iSAMS which has made our reporting and assessment systems electronic, and being involved in that transition has enabled me to have input to the direction of frequency and methods of assessment and reporting.

I have found the whole process of formal qualification beneficial, and its intersection with my role as deputy head has mostly been helpful. My view has moved on from thinking that either one can teach or one can't. I still believe that providing the magnetism to draw pupils to what you are talking about is at the heart of it (as my former Headmaster used to say: "Don't look at me; look the way I'm looking"). However, acquiring QTS has shown me that there are many ways to achieve this pull and almost everything can be improved with reflection and practice.

References
[1]The Training and Development Agency Guidance for New Qualified Teachers lists five themes for induction:
(i) developing professional and constructive relationships;
(ii) working within the law and frameworks;
(iii) professional knowledge and understanding;
(iv) professional skills;
(v) developing practice.

Chapter 3

Responsibilities and rewards: advice on starting out

Louise Moelwyn-Hughes

It will come as no surprise to those of you who are embarking upon a teaching career that, as in most walks of life, alongside the many and varied rewards of the job there will inevitably come significant responsibility. With responsibility comes complexity: what is the best course of action for all concerned; what is the appropriate response to any given situation; when is it right to hand over issues to others to deal with and for you to assume more of a back seat; to what extent should you compromise, and to what extent and to what end should you pursue your cause?

As an NQT, and perhaps also a young member of staff, you may find yourself perfectly placed to view an institution and its ways with a fresh pair of eyes; to understand some of the frustrations which students might feel about the seemingly stifling or dated rules and regulations and to have much in common with the student body with which you are now engaging.

This can indeed be a valuable pastoral tool: one which can be used to good effect for the benefit of both student and school. There should be no senior management team which is unaware of the untapped pastoral potential of younger members of staff. Frequently it happens that a student makes a quiet approach to a younger member of staff and asks for advice on what might seem a peculiarly dry question, such as the niceties of Latin grammar or how to begin that essay, which the unfeeling and, of course, older English teacher unsympathetically set.

It is certainly not always the case (but it does seem to happen with notable regularity) that students, especially teenagers, will turn to a younger member of staff for help and guidance as they feel that, in some way, they share common ground. It is true to say that, for the most part, younger teachers may have only recently escaped the straitjacket of public examinations themselves. Students will realise that young teachers, perhaps more than any other adult known to them, will share that maelstrom of feelings which arises from knowing that education is a necessity and a passport to an exciting career, whilst at the same time being acutely aware that there are other pressing issues in life: matters which the world of education and school might seem to them to obstruct or interrupt.

In such a situation, the NQT may find that (s)he has effectively been put into the powerful position of having the ear of an individual (or, indeed, of part or all of a class). At this point it is important to recognise that, enjoyable and perhaps flattering though it may be to be awarded the attention of one's students, great caution must be exercised. Common sense must of course rule the day. Not allowing students to become over-reliant upon you as an individual is vitally important.

You should certainly steer clear of making a student feel uncomfortable about his or her approach, but at the same time you should be very clear that you are there to elucidate and educate, not to befriend. Try wherever possible to avoid the potentially compromising situation of teaching one-to-one, and be careful to choose a venue where there will be sufficient passing traffic for both you and the student not to feel isolated. In other words, avoid dealing with a student behind a closed door unless it is absolutely unavoidable.

Be wary, too, of students asking exclusively for your time, and try to open revision explanatory sessions up to others in the group. If a student is making over-frequent visits to you, however well-meaning they may appear, look for ways of opening the situation up and inviting other pupils to join you: it will send the signal to the student that your intention is to teach, not to form a personal attachment or confer preferential treatment.

It may surprise you to discover just how quickly, if a student begins to form an unhealthy interest in a teacher, the other students will pick up on it. Be aware of the fact that they will be extremely interested in how the situation progresses and don't lose sight of the fact that they will judge you on how you deal with the matter.

If, on the other hand, a pupil approaches you with a genuine pastoral concern, you must again use careful judgement as to how you handle the situation. You may get the feeling that it has taken great trust and courage for a student to seek you out to divulge sensitive information. It is easy under these circumstances to allow yourself to be swept away by the moment, either rushing to give advice to one in need, or indeed to sympathise to the point where you are at risk of becoming a character in the narrative.

You need to be aware that anything you say may well be repeated by an emotional student and that, with many teenagers in particular, wars are fought and decided in what could be a matter of hours. Your spontaneous comments about other students, members of staff, or indeed parents may be repeated out of context and could return to haunt you.

The key, of course, to any potential disclosure from a student is to try to pre-empt its arrival in one key respect. Even if you are completely in the dark as to the possible content of the disclosure, be prepared for the question of confidentiality to be posed. The quickly uttered statement "I need to tell you something, but you can't tell anyone", followed by the deep intake of breath signifying that the student is about to launch into a difficult monologue, must be punctuated by an interjection from you.

Of course, the information may indeed be serious, warranting adult help or intervention, so without scaring the pupil away, you must get across the point that you cannot *guarantee* to keep information to yourself, and that you may judge that if you did, it would be harmful to the student or to a third party. This isn't a personal preference or an option: it is quite simply an approach which *all* teachers should follow.

It is usually best to leave the student to consider what you have said before suggesting (s)he visits other professionals – for example, a school nurse, a chaplain or a counsellor – for advice. I have found that in most situations the student is actually aware that you cannot keep sensitive information confidential, and that in deciding to make an approach, (s)he has reached a point where (s)he is willing to disclose it and positively wants to be guided to the next level.

If the student insists that confidentiality is needed, it might be worth asking what the broad nature of the problem is and then attempting to encourage an approach to a professional who is better placed to help. Keep in mind the fact that if a student carries on to elaborate upon a situation or incident, it is likely that you are being confided in because (s)he wants sympathy and advice. Listening is of the essence here and, if the issue is not of a child protection nature (see chapter 4), offer sensible steps and guidance as far as you feel confident and competent to do so.

Opening up a problem so that you are not locked into being the only adult who has information is crucial. Even in respect of information which is relatively straightforward and manageable, it is always a good idea to involve the student's tutor or a head of year so that those who care directly for the student have at least some outline idea of what is happening, and also so that you have protected yourself if the situation deteriorates.

If the problem is complicated and you do not feel entirely comfortable with it, it is best to encourage the student to speak with other members of staff or specialist professionals, perhaps offering to accompany them, especially if the adult you are recommending is not one known to the student. The expertise and support of those around you will help to ensure that the student is given the best advice and guidance, and also that you are not isolated and therefore open to criticism or blame.

For the most part, however, your life as a teacher is likely to revolve around more routine, even straightforward, issues. You are, for example, facing the sometimes daunting prospect of being left alone with a whole class for the first time, with the knowledge that you will have to keep its members occupied for a whole year and achieve something worthwhile and tangible by the end of it.

Make sure that you are dressed appropriately for the work which you have come to do. A surprising number of new teachers (including some of the very best prospects) misjudge this, most of them occasionally rather than every day. Even in an age when people generally dress down much more than in the past, it will help your authority if you are dressed authoritatively – not expensively, nor for the fashion catwalk, nor stiflingly power-dressed – and certainly not provocatively or in a way which causes your pupils to think that you have forgotten that in age terms you are no longer a pupil yourself.

Being minded to maintain reasonably conservative attire, whilst not quite subscribing to the Miss Jean Brodie look, will mean that the focus of attention in the classroom is not on you, but rather on the task in hand. Year 10 and 11 pupils in particular need little to stir their imaginations: you will know the rest, or be able to work it out for yourself!

Be firm and make sure that you set your boundaries early on. Make your demands on the class realistic, so that you can maintain consistency throughout the year. Oddly, despite the fact that you may suddenly feel very alone when confronted with a sea of faces – some waiting expectantly for you to say something momentous and others seemingly oblivious to the fact that you are there at all – far from being united as a solid group of (say) 24, you do in fact have 24 individuals sitting in front of you, each of whom may well feel as separate from any notion of being part of a cohesive group as you do.

Try to banish the thought that all eyes are on you. In reality, that may be the case, but there is also a sense in which each pupil will feel as if you are watching him or her; students will often feel as if they are as alone in the classroom as you do. Be sure to take control of the situation quickly and get the students listening and on task. Make sure that your lesson has a strong and confident opening statement: hanging around, or beating about the bush, will engender general conversation in the class and will turn individuals' attention away from you and take them well and truly off topic.

Be clear and simple in your instructions and allow the students to have confidence in the fact that you know the direction in which you are taking them, and that you are comfortable with and interested in the subject matter yourself. Students are often looking to be reassured that you and they are doing the right thing.

The golden rule, especially with bright students, is never to pretend that you know something when you don't – teenagers tend to have a sixth sense about these things and if they spot that you are being defensively inventive, it will simply instigate further questioning, perhaps with the purpose of leading you to contradiction. Students can be merciless in this regard, so it is best to say calmly and confidently that the question is a good one, and either to undertake to revisit the question next lesson having discovered the answer yourself, or to set the individual or class an investigative task to report back. To be seen not to know the answer to everything will not be viewed as a crime to students or to colleagues, but to try to cover up what you don't know will surely cause them to question your ability – both in terms of your mastery of the subject matter and your effectiveness as a teacher.

Although the working hours of a teacher, especially in the boarding sector, may seem to those beyond the system to be reasonable in length and the periods of holiday generous in the extreme, it is often forgotten that being a teacher extends well beyond what takes place in the classroom, and indeed beyond the working day itself. Being a steady and responsible figure, a role model in many ways, is what many teachers aspire to be, whether it comes naturally or not.

You may at one stage or another in a long teaching career come to consider practically every public aspect of your life through the lens of your job. The activities in which you involve yourself at the weekends can be affected to an extent by your position in a school – in a small town, mixing in the same social spaces as your own students might prove both stifling for you and difficult to marry with your day job.

There is one aspect of a teacher's life which, although extreme and in some ways forbidding, it is sensible to spell out. Periodically there are press stories about teachers caught in compromising and complicated relationships with pupils. Understandably, we all think that this is something that will only happen to someone else and could never happen to us, but you should be aware that some very promising teachers have got themselves into difficulties in the past – sometimes simply as a result of being among the most gifted, charismatic and popular members of their profession.

In legal terms, where a relationship of trust (*eg* teaching) exists, allowing a relationship to develop in a way that *might* lead later to a sexual relationship is wrong. In child protection matters, this idea of encouraging things to develop tends to be known as 'grooming', but the principle underlying both these things is much the same, and what precisely constitutes it in teaching has no hard and fast legal definition: you should always err on the side of caution.

It is unacceptable for a member of staff to have *any* kind of sexual or intimate relationships/contact with a pupil of *any* age or to encourage such relationships/contact. The Sexual Offences Act 2003 makes it a criminal offence for a teacher to involve a pupil under 18 in a sexual activity, but it goes further in deeming such relationships/contact as a breach of trust and professional standards, even where the pupil is over 18.

Why do I spell this out? This chapter cannot cover every eventuality, but some examples will suffice from which you can draw general principles. Any teacher can face a situation in which he or she is given opportunities to meet pupils in social situations, especially in boarding schools. In day schools, these tend to be fewer, but they range from casual encounters at the weekend to some set-piece events: one example is the parent who invites a young member of staff to an 18th birthday party, partly as a 'thank you' for earlier pastoral encouragement, or mentoring in the classroom or on the games field. Both types of school have leavers' balls or similar events.

There can be no hard and fast rules in such situations except one: never forget that, as a teacher, you are in a position of trust, legally as well as in other ways, by virtue of your position and the work you undertake. Above all, keep in mind that the law expects that those in positions of trust will exercise responsibility as a consequence of the power they have over those they teach and/or care for. You are wise to live your social life away and apart from your pupils.

Where the party is concerned, you will probably be flattered to be asked: it is a compliment to you. However, you should also be sure not to be naive. Try to find out more about the nature of the event, and assess the risk. How visible a parent presence will there be? Is it to be a sit-down meal inside, or a less formal event outside? Seek advice from those in the school more senior than you; it is all too possible that, through the actions of others and/or what you see of their behaviour, you may be put in a situation which is at least embarrassing, and at worst professionally compromising.

In respect of the leavers' ball, it is good that staff (including young staff) support such events; good, too, that schools are concerned to give pupils a rousing send-off, and that they and staff can say "goodbye" to each other after so many hours of mutual endeavour in and beyond the classroom. Never forget, though, that in the eyes of the law, *all* your A level students (including a few who are not yet 18) are still members of the school. Resist the temptation to go on after the ball to celebrate elsewhere with your leavers.

Taking care over your use of the internet is sensible. In particular, consider your intelligent management of entries posted on to sites such as Facebook, where a compromising photograph of your more frivolous self might later cause you endless headaches in the classroom. Always keeping a healthy distance between you and your students has got to be good advice. It is true that you may well, as a young teacher, visit similar social haunts and enjoy pastimes similar to many of your older students, but remember that your remit is not to befriend, but to educate.

I well remember a young teacher trying his level best to win the favour of members of his class, of whom I was one, only to find that the novelty soon wore off among the students, leaving the teacher disliked by the boys for allegedly giving preferential treatment to the girls and being equally disliked by the girls as they began to see his interest in them as rather sad and pathetic. The key is to prove an interesting and vibrant personality through the medium of teaching, not through pandering for popularity.

Students will respect, and possibly admire, a teacher who sets clear boundaries, who is fair, and who gets on with the job of educating. Students will have access to many people throughout their lives whom they can befriend and so will teachers. I am firmly of the belief that there is little to be gained from them befriending each other.

I am conscious that I run the risk of sounding excessively prohibitive in detailing all that a trainee teacher must take care *not* to do. We all find ourselves tested at some stage in our careers but, in essence, the majority of adults will easily grasp what is needed to succeed inside and outside the classroom. Many of the suggestions above are indeed simply ones of common sense. The key is to learn good practice early on and to stick with it. Conversing regularly with other members of staff will prove hugely beneficial, and bouncing ideas off each other is reciprocally helpful. Beyond dry teaching manuals there is a huge wealth of expertise, ideas and inventiveness within every staff room, and you will quickly find that any query which you bring to discussion will be met with a raft of possible ways forward.

If you take the time to tap into this free human resource, you will undoubtedly find yourself armed with a range of options for any given situation and will be urged not to shoulder the burden alone. It is rare for there to be just one quick fix to problems, especially those of a pastoral nature, but soon you will see that your input to discussion will mean that you are proving to be a valuable resource for other members of staff who are faced with exactly the same conundrums each day.

It is important to bear in mind that there will be few situations which will not have been touched upon or heard of before by more experienced members of the school staff and, although it is right and proper that you should find pathways through problem areas in ways which feel right for you, you should never fear speaking up to find out how others might proceed.

Above all, if you follow your common sense and take note of the advice in this chapter, you should find that teaching is a life rich in rewarding returns as well as responsibilities. Ours is a job which includes the ability and influence to shape and transform young lives: even though we should always take it seriously, we should also rejoice in it.

Chapter 4

Child protection and your protection

Amanda Triccas

In spite of the fact that some of the perceptions of children educated in the independent sector are that they are privileged, even pampered, the reality is that – like their state school counterparts – they are just as vulnerable to abuse. While it is important not to jump to the most dire conclusion (especially after your compulsory child protection training, when your antennae are particularly attuned to signs of abuse), no child's articulated concern should ever be ignored, or brushed aside. Above all, don't be afraid to seek advice from those more experienced than you.

Although teachers have always kept an eye on the wellbeing of their pupils, they have been integrated more formally into the network of children's services since 2004. The process of redefining teachers' professional responsibilities and workloads and the shocking revelations from the Victoria Climbié case led to the government policy *Every Child Matters* (ECM).[1]

Under this initiative, a growing set of obligations and initiatives have been developed. Teachers are obliged under the Children Act 2004[2] to implement measures which help children achieve the following outcomes:

- to be healthy;
- to stay safe;
- to enjoy and achieve;
- to make a positive contribution;
- to achieve economic wellbeing.

You will touch upon ECM issues frequently throughout your induction period but one central plank of the policy is the safeguarding of children and young people.

Teachers are part of a 'workforce' comprising various agencies in the wider community – including social services, health professionals and governors, as well as parents and carers. Teachers do not bear full responsibility for all aspects of child protection but, as a piece of the child welfare jigsaw, they are as important as other agencies.

NQTs need to contribute effectively, working collaboratively to enable the progress of young people. They should prove their understanding of their distinct role in the workforce and the expertise they bring to it. As well as pastoral work, subject learning must be planned to meet individual children's needs. Teachers must also realise that child protection initiatives are constantly evolving, so it is important to review developments regularly.

Your school is responsible for providing ongoing training which enables you to be a positive contributor to the workforce. In most cases, that learning process may be more theoretical than practical. An NQT may well not encounter a child at risk and may therefore worry about his or her ability to provide evidence that (s)he has contributed to the development of this core standard.

Child protection standards

There are Core standards under 'professional knowledge and understanding' explicitly mentioning safeguarding issues:

C21 Know when to draw on the expertise of colleagues, such as those with responsibility for the safeguarding of children and young people and special educational needs and disabilities, and to refer to sources of information, advice and support from external agencies.

C22 Know the current legal requirements, national policies and guidance on the safeguarding and promotion of the wellbeing of children and young people.

C23 Know the local arrangements concerning the safeguarding of children and young people.

C24 Know how to identify potential child abuse or neglect and follow safeguarding procedures.

C25 Know how to identify and support children and young people whose progress, development or wellbeing is affected by changes or difficulties in their personal circumstances, and when to refer them to colleagues for specialist support.

C37 (a) Establish a purposeful and safe learning environment which complies with current legal requirements, national policies and guidance on the safeguarding and wellbeing of children and young people, so that learners feel secure and sufficiently confident to make an active contribution to learning and to the school. (b) Make use of the local arrangements concerning the safeguarding of children and young people.

Guidance outlined in the Education Act 2002[3] requires all school employees to have child protection training every three years. This training includes the legal requirements, national policies and local arrangements as well as advice about identifying and reporting abuse, thereby satisfying these standards.

While best practice is to provide this as part of whole-school INSET, it is crucial that this training is provided for all NQTs, ideally as soon as possible after you join the staff. You should bring this up with your induction tutor if is not clear when this will happen. Lack of safeguarding training will make it much harder to evidence these standards.

Drawing on the expertise of colleagues

Schools should have a designated teacher with specific responsibility for co-ordinating safeguarding policies, practices and training. You must know the name of this person from the day you join the school. There ought to be a nominated governor for child protection as well as a relevant school policy which is available to staff, parents and governors.

As well as the SENCO mentioned in the standards, the school pastoral structure will also provide form teachers, heads of year and those providing medical services, all of whom it would be appropriate to approach to discuss the wellbeing of a child. However, if you are worried that a child is being abused, neglected or in danger of harm, do not feel inhibited about going straight to the designated teacher with your concerns. It is always best to avoid risks where a child's welfare is concerned.

What is abuse and neglect?

There are quite clear guidelines on this which you will have looked at during initial teacher training. Websites such as that run by Kidscape[4] and TeacherNet[5] give plenty of information and are updated regularly.

You may never be sure if something you spot is a result of abuse. All the more reason, therefore, to realise that you are part of the safeguarding jigsaw and that you must pass concerns on to those who may be in a better position to investigate further. You may have spotted that a child has recently been coming to school sporting fresh bruises. This may well turn out be a result of his or her recently-acquired skateboard. No one is going to be annoyed with you for raising the issue. It may just as well have been the result of his or her recently-acquired step-brother. It is not up to you to investigate and solve the problem yourself. Pass the concern on.

Sometimes teachers speak of a 'hunch' that all is not well and using emotional intelligence to inform one's relationship-building in the school environment is central to becoming an experienced professional. While it may seem rather daunting to approach a senior colleague with a concern based on a hunch, never be deterred: your intervention may be the turning-point that saves a child.

Disclosure

Although abused children often try to hide the evidence, in a few cases a child may make a direct disclosure to you. This will bring your part in the network of welfare workers into sharp relief, and the responsibility upon your shoulders will be immense. Naturally you will not have time to look up advice about how to manage this, so any good child protection INSET will reiterate best practice when dealing with this situation and remind you of the following points:

- Stay calm and react appropriately. Avoiding looking distressed, however harrowing the details. Nevertheless, do not look as if you are uninterested, or worse that you do not believe what you are being told. Ensure the pupil knows that (s)he is being taken seriously: otherwise (s)he might clam up and the ability to help may be delayed.

- Respond immediately. Do not tell the child to come back later because you have to teach or that you have a meeting. The moment will be lost and the child may not come forward again. If necessary, alert a colleague that someone will have to organise cover or convey your apologies. The welfare of the child is always paramount.

- Be reassuring by appearing calm and therefore reliable. Resist any temptation to cuddle the pupil or to pass judgement on the person who has been upsetting them.

- Do not make promises that you will keep this to yourself. You must inform the pupil that you may need to tell someone who can help them.

- Listen more than you speak. It is especially important not to ask leading questions or to put ideas into the child's mind. Do not offer alternative explanations or excuses for an abuser's behaviour. However, it is good to try to summarise back to the child what (s)he has just said. This allows you to check that you are hearing what (s)he is trying to say and also reassures the child that you are being supportive. However, take care not to elaborate or sensationalise. Use language that is appropriate to the child's age, background and level of understanding to ensure that the child is not confused.

- You may need to get the child to a place of safety or medical attention. This may involve calling an ambulance immediately.

- Make detailed notes about the conversation as soon as possible afterwards. Make a note of the date, time and place and try to use the child's words as far as possible. Sign this document and pass immediately to the school's designated person. You may need to give evidence formally, so make sure your notes are comprehensive and lucid.

- Alert the designated person immediately. It is now their case. Follow their advice carefully. Do not pass information to others not involved in the case, for example by informal staff room chat.

What if your concerns are not acted upon?

Child protection trainers will always advise you to act immediately on your concerns. However, you also need to act with tact and care. You may not always be aware of measures being taken by the safeguarding workforce once a case has come their way. Do not assume that because you are not receiving detailed feedback, the matter is not being taken seriously.

However, if you feel that your concerns have been dismissed out of hand by the designated person and if you feel that you are not getting a satisfactory explanation, your responsibility is always towards the well-being of the child and you should speak directly to the Head. If the Head is unwilling to act, the governor with responsibility for child protection should be alerted. In extreme cases, the local authority can be contacted directly. Taking this step may be rather unpopular with your school leadership team but, of course, child protection is not a popularity contest and the child's needs will always come before any other considerations. However, with a well-trained designated person, this problem should not arise.

If you are aware of allegations against a colleague, realise that as well as discharging its responsibilities towards the child, it will also be necessary for the institution to manage the public implications of the case so your discretion will be crucial.

The special demands of boarding

Put bluntly, the extended contact hours in boarding schools give more opportunity to spot any abuse. You will be more likely to see a student in a variety of clothes such as nightwear and casual dress which might allow you to spot if (s)he is injured or underweight, for example. Similarly, the teacher who is with their students 24 hours a day occupies a subtly different role, *in loco parentis* not only legally and physically but also, to a degree, emotionally. Disclosure may be easier for a child with a great deal of trust in their head of house. The same advice as above still stands, however, and the designated person should be contacted when there is concern.

Your influence over a dependent child is potentially great and you must take care to exercise this appropriately. Particular care must be taken when entering sleeping areas and bathrooms. Avoid being alone with a student and aim to find more neutral areas to talk one-to-one. A teacher who is of a different gender to the pupils at a single-sex boarding school will need guidance on access to dormitories and so forth. You may need to attend to a child in the middle of the night, so ensure that your nightwear is appropriately demure.

Boarding school staff need to be even more emotionally intelligent than most, and your ability to judge appropriate pastoral responses will develop with time and experience. Seek out a colleague to mentor you and if you are ever in doubt about a course of action, get a second opinion.

Routine safeguarding

Much safeguarding of young people in the school environment comes from everyday awareness of health and safety procedures. The induction of all new staff should include training in fire drill and the use of fire equipment, as well as more specific safety guidance for staff working in areas of particular concern such as science, design technology and physical education. Make sure that you know where to find the health and safety documentation for your school – often a handbook or a set of policies. If you teach a subject in which it is important to devise risk assessments for activities within your scheme of work, make sure that your subject mentor is managing this with you.

Educational visits

Some of the more publicised cases of children coming to harm while in the care of a school arise from educational visits. As an NQT you should aim to accompany a range of visits during your induction period: a local day visit; an evening trip; a residential visit. Observe experienced colleagues managing issues such as pupils' safety on public transport, on public highways, on private coaches.

Be aware of how to work with the medical staff at school so that you can safeguard pupils with conditions such as diabetes, epilepsy and asthma. Know which medical equipment needs to be carried by staff and get training for operating an EpiPen in case it ever becomes necessary. Meanwhile the catering department needs to be brought into the loop if it is required to provide packed lunches for pupils with food allergies and other dietary requirements. Male and female teachers may have different responsibilities managing residential visits and, in some girls' schools, male teachers may not be allowed to accompany visits.

You may have to organise a trip yourself before the end of induction. If your school has an educational visits coordinator, work closely with them to make sure that you are following procedures. Writing a risk assessment is an important part of the planning process as you anticipate the sort of things which might go wrong. You should then consider in advance how to mitigate them.

Safeguarding yourself and colleagues

Education unions note an increasing number of accusations against teaching professionals, the vast majority of which turn out to be unfounded or exaggerated.[6] Most accusations are of physical abuse, but sexual misconduct can sometimes be alleged. The consequences of such cases can be devastating as Heads have the right (though not the duty) to suspend the accused pending investigation.

It is therefore important that you are aware of how to safeguard yourself and colleagues in this respect and there are a number of ways to do this. Maintain professional boundaries. Do not give out your address, personal (as opposed to school) email address, mobile or home landline number to students or parents unless your school requires this. It is good practice to record all communications which come through these channels if you feel that they are in some way threatening or compromising. Never give out similar information relating to a colleague.

Do not communicate with current pupils using social networking sites. Realise that former pupils may be communicating with current pupils on these sites, thereby allowing all to read what you post. A good rule of thumb is to post only comments which you would be happy for your employer to read. Do not comment upon your current pupils on such sites, however innocent your remark may seem.

Do not gossip inappropriately about students with other pupils or with colleagues. Similarly do not discuss other colleagues with students. It is easy to pass on personal information which they would rather not have disclosed. For some staff, the fact that they are married or in a relationship is a matter of complete privacy to them and it is not your business to pass that on.

Do not socialise with current pupils. Some teachers (and not always younger ones) enjoy feeling part of this youthful crowd, but it should be avoided. This is even more important in locations where alcohol (or drugs) may be available. If alcohol is served at a school event, it may be school policy to allow students to consume a moderate amount but you need to be responsible for making sure that 'moderate' is adhered to.

Teachers are often advised not to be alone in a room with a child. This is often impracticable for those who routinely work from their offices, such as the leadership or medical teams, and for instrumental or language teachers delivering one-to-one tuition. You can leave the door ajar or make sure that the room has a window in the door and take advice from other colleagues who work in similar circumstances. Avoid giving a child a lift in your car.

Physical contact with pupils should be minimal, needs-led and appropriate. Grasping a child's arm firmly might be considered assault by a litigious parent. Comfort a distressed child with words rather than hugs. In the extreme case of physical force being used to restrain a child who is endangering him or herself or others, make a statement of events to your line manager as soon as possible after the incident.[7]

Be extremely careful with images of children. Where photographs or video footage are used as part of learning or assessment, make sure that your line manager is aware of what you are doing and avoid putting these images on to your private computer. Don't leave them on the system longer than necessary.

Always remember that modern technology means that none of us is immune from appearing as inadvertent stars in videos on YouTube and similar sites. We have no control over what is posted: of course you are going to need to let your hair down from time to time, but be aware of where you are and what you are doing.

Remember that even if footage of you dancing drunkenly in the Trafalgar Square fountains with your pants on your head might not lead to a formal sanction, the damage to your reputation may be hard to undo – and you don't necessarily want to gain a reputation with Year 8 as Knickerman – or woman. Damaged reputations cannot easily be rebuilt and the cliché of 'no smoke without fire' remains as potent as ever.

References

[1] www.dcsf.gov.uk/everychildmatters
[2] Children Act 2004 c.31
[3] Education Act 2002 c.32
[4] www.kidscape.org.uk/professionals/childabuse.shtml
[5] www.teachernet.gov.uk/wholeschool/familyandcommunity/childprotection/usefulinformation/definitionsofabuse/
[6] *Report* – the magazine from the Association of Teachers and Lecturers, April 2009, p.10.
[7] www.teachernet.gov.uk/_doc/12187/ACFD89B.pdf

Chapter 5

Good classroom practice

Nick Fraser

Preparation

At the front of my classroom there is a poster which exhorts pupils to remember the five Ps: 'Proper preparation prevents poor performance.' This applies to teachers at all stages of their career, but particularly to those entering the profession. Preparation of all aspects of the job – the room, the learning materials, pupils' exercise books to be returned and the lesson plan – reduces the expenditure of unnecessary energy and alleviates anxiety.

Lesson plans should not simply incorporate a sequence of random tasks to fill the period and keep pupils busy and quiet, of course. Nor should they be based predominantly on what we intend to teach or 'cover' but should be constructed around what we want the pupils to *learn*. A good lesson plan will, therefore, consider what the *pupils* will do and how the activities of a lesson will further their knowledge and understanding. It can also be helpful to plan lessons around key questions which we want pupils to be able to answer by the end of the period.

Consideration should also be given to the shape or 'architecture' of a lesson. A common approach is to include a starter activity, which reviews the learning of the previous lesson or anticipates an aspect of future learning, and then to devote the majority of the lesson to activities which promote new learning or provide consolidation.

It is helpful to build in time at the end of lessons for the purpose of review. As another of my classroom posters reminds us: 'Trying to learn without reviewing is like trying to fill a bath without putting the plug in.'[1] The propensity of humans to forget 80% of what they have learned within 24 hours, the so-called Ebbinghaus effect, is a sobering thought and one worth bearing in mind when we plan our lessons: we must provide regular opportunities for our pupils to revisit previously-learned material if we truly want to help them remember what we have taught. Good teachers are similarly aware that learning is all about seeking and securing connections and devising links – not only to prior learning but also to other topics, other subjects and everyday life.

The 'starter – main activity – review' structure of a lesson is not the only possibility, of course: indeed it is advisable to modify the structure of our lessons according to the day and the time of day: the last lessons in the afternoon require special care, for instance. Wise teachers also vary the type of activities included in each of their day's lessons so that some include calm, quiet activities and some involve more expenditure of energy on the teacher's part.

No teacher can deliver 'all singing, all dancing' lessons for eight consecutive periods, five days a week, for any length of time without running the risk of rapid burnout! Finally, our planning should anticipate the most stressful parts of the school year, such as those where report writing looms large, and ensure that those times of year do not clash with the peak demands of the work from our classes.

Classroom management
Good classroom management is absolutely crucial for effective learning and teaching to take place, and it is something which all teachers should continue to refine throughout their careers. Whilst accepting that there is no such thing as perfect classroom management, and that all teachers will bring their own unique personality to the classroom, it is, nevertheless, true that effective – and enjoyable – teaching is largely based on a productive working relationship between the teacher and the pupils. Good classroom management ensures that pupils have a safe environment in which to think and express themselves and, over time, it allows individual teaching styles to flourish.

All pupils need – and, either openly or secretly, like – to know the boundaries, and time devoted to setting clear parameters in our initial encounters with classes is time well spent. There is no magic formula for effective classroom control; but there are some universal principles which may confidently be applied.

First, considerable thought should be given to seating arrangements. Some teachers insist that pupils sit in alphabetical order, at least initially. Others decide where each pupil will sit on the basis of prior knowledge or advice from colleagues. No teacher should feel obliged to allow pupils to sit beside friends if this is likely to be counterproductive: they spend plenty of time with classmates of their own choosing outside the classroom and must, ultimately at any rate, learn to work with others even if they do not have a natural affinity with them.

Even if pupils are allowed to sit where they please initially, it should be made clear to them that where they sit is a privilege rather than a right, and that it is the teacher's prerogative to move a pupil if this is required. Whichever approach is adopted (and there is no single right answer), it is undeniably true that 'care over initial seating contributes more than any other single action to the management of the class in subsequent weeks'.[2]

Secondly, rapid mastery of pupils' names is essential for effective classroom management, not least since it can, in the teacher's mind, break down a challenging class into manageable – and likeable – individuals. It is well worth making a conscious effort to memorise pupils' names as early as possible and certainly within the first couple of lessons. There are several techniques which can be employed to ease this process:

(a) If possible, study class lists in advance. Many schools will have a database which makes it possible to print lists of names accompanied by pupils' photos. This enables teachers to put as many names to faces as possible before even meeting a class for the first time. It is also advisable to check with colleagues how difficult names should be pronounced, as this can avoid a potentially explosive first encounter with a child who takes umbrage at having his or her name mispronounced.

(b) Create or have pupils make cards which clearly show their names and can be propped up on their desks for the first few lessons until such time as the teacher knows the names of all members of the class.

(c) Use pupils' names as much as possible when asking a question, thanking them for a response, giving out books or returning exercise books. Take every opportunity to talk to pupils on a one-to-one basis, using their name several times in each discussion.

(d) Create small cards with the name of each pupil in the class on a separate card. When asking pupils to answer questions, use these cards to determine who answers – and make sure that you consciously notice which pupil responds. Incidentally, the use of such cards to decide randomly which pupils answer which questions can increase pupils' attention, since no pupil knows who will be called upon to respond at any particular point. This avoids the undesirable classroom situation whereby there is 'a small discussion group surrounded by sleepy onlookers'.[3]

(e) Devise a seating plan showing which pupil sits where, and refer to it for the first few lessons without becoming dependent upon it. Over-use of a seating plan can break up the flow of a lesson and encourage laziness in you *vis-à-vis* learning pupils' names quickly.

Thirdly, a teacher's expectations should be made clear from the outset. These should be simple, reasonable and stated clearly: possibly displayed on the classroom wall or stuck in pupils' exercise books and referred to often, particularly in the initial stages.

In behavioural matters, each individual teacher must work out for him or herself how much should be tolerated and what should be accepted; but there are certain universal rules and principles which are relevant for every teacher in every classroom. We should never accept talking during a declared silent session or while we are addressing the class. There is no point in talking over pupils' voices, and though this might take some courage, patience and persistence initially, this rule must be emphasised early on.

Furthermore, we should all take pupils to task for homework which is not done, and good record keeping is crucial here also. It is advisable always to get cross with latecomers or with pupils who produce sub-standard work.

This can all sound dull and somewhat onerous; but it is true that 'initial fuss reduces subsequent fuss'[4] and that if we are firm and well organised initially, it is possible to create a more relaxed and friendlier atmosphere later in the term. It should never be forgotten that, no matter how much some may protest, pupils thrive on systems and consistent routines: creating orderly, methodical classroom procedures allows productive relationships and effective learning to flourish.

New teachers are advised not to aim for an overfriendly rapport with pupils too early in the term, nor to settle for lower standards in order to make quick but temporary gains in their relationships. The old adage 'don't smile before Christmas' may sound too draconian for classrooms in the 21st century, but the principle whereby new teachers aim for optimum relationships with pupils by the end of the first term (rather than by the end of the first week) remains sound.

The establishment of rules and expectations presupposes, of course, that there must be consequences for pupils who choose to flaunt or disregard them. It is vital that all teachers new to a school familiarise themselves with departmental and school sanctions. It is often felt to be good practice for sanctions to be graduated, with pupils knowing in advance what this approach to discipline means: for example when dealing with missing homework, the first occasion might simply mean a warning with the requirement that the work be produced the next day; the second occasion might warrant an extra task to be completed in addition to the original and submitted the next day; the third occasion might mean that a referral slip or demerit be issued, thus involving a pupil's tutor or the head of department.

Each school is different, however, and it is advisable to discuss school and departmental policies with colleagues before term begins so as to know which sanctions are appropriate for specific types of misbehaviour. It might also be worthwhile planning 'what if' scenarios in advance with colleagues, in order to be prepared for how best to react to common behavioural issues, so that these can be handled calmly and knowledgeably, should the need arise. When sanctions are required, criticism should be specific and clear, and should refer to the behaviour, not the person.

Effective classroom management does not merely rely on the use of sanctions, however. The vast majority of pupils respond very positively to praise and reward. Good teachers are adept at finding opportunities to 'catch them being good' and to reinforce positive behaviours. Many schools run systems of commendations and positive referrals in tandem with official sanctions. Moreover, the use of humour to defuse instances of misbehaviour or moments of tension is a technique which is well worth honing and incorporating into one's repertoire of behaviour management strategies.

Finally, much classroom management relies on that indefinable quality: *presence*. Certain steps can be taken to ensure that teachers possess this from the outset. For instance, for those of us fortunate enough to have our own classroom, time and care should be devoted to creating an attractive, well-organised and workmanlike space. This makes clear our pride in, and care for, the classroom and commitment to learning, and these immediately bring our subject alive and encourage interest. Effective displays can make a statement about the subjects taught in that room and can also reflect a teacher's personal interests.

Other possibilities include motivational material, reasons for learning a particular subject, and displays to aid learning such as keywords or strategies for developing particular skills. It is certainly true that pupils tend to behave better in a well-kept, aesthetically pleasing room which is individual in character. Wall space devoted to the display of pupils' work can also be a great motivator. In addition to decorating our working spaces in order to create a sense of presence, we should also organise the tables and chairs in such a way as to facilitate movement around the room.

By walking around, scanning and maintaining an oversight of all classroom activity, we automatically command greater presence than if we remain rooted to one spot at the front of the room, particularly if this looks like a defensive position behind the teacher's desk.

Finally, we should ensure that our presence and ensuing classroom management are based on clear professional standards. As the adult in the relationship, we should model the behaviours we wish to see in the youngsters in our charge, and work patiently at relationships which are built on a platform of mutual respect.

Resources

Good planning requires not only a clear sense of what pupils will learn in the course of a lesson (or series of lessons), but also a knowledge of activities in which they will need to engage to meet those objectives. In order to provide a varied diet of learning tasks which are engaging, motivating and effective, we need to amass a range of resources for the myriad topics which we teach.

This varied repertoire will include reading material, writing tasks, worksheets, visual material, audio material and, increasingly, digital material. This may understandably seem particularly daunting to teachers starting out on their careers, for whom the onus of preparation can weigh heavily in the initial stages.

There are, however, steps which can be taken to alleviate this burden. First and foremost, we should acquaint ourselves as much as possible with what is already available, so as not to reinvent the wheel. This can be achieved, for example, by spending time in departments before the first day of teaching, finding out what already exists in departmental offices and files. Good schemes of work should also indicate which resources are available within the department for particular topics, and some may well have digital material stored on a shared resource area on the school's network or intranet.

Time spent familiarising oneself with what is available online can also be beneficial: the *Times Educational Supplement*'s resource section, the National Grid for Learning, the London and the Birmingham Grids for Learning[5] (to name but a few) contain many useful resources. The social bookmarking site del.icio.us makes it possible to save all useful links in one place and, as an added advantage, indicates how many other users have bookmarked the same sites and allows us to navigate to their saved links – this can lead to many profitable discoveries!

There is one caveat, however: it is extremely easy to spend more time searching for materials on the web and following interesting links than it would take to create a new resource or locate one in existing departmental areas. As in all things, a balance needs to be struck.

Another important resource is, of course, people: departmental colleagues and teachers in different departments and schools can all be a source of useful advice and support. There will also be subject associations and online discussion groups to which all teachers can subscribe, and these can provide ideas, materials, hints and details of events, courses and conferences. Moreover, time spent observing other colleagues in the classroom, including those of different subjects, is always instructive and will often generate a wealth of ideas, as well as demonstrating a range of approaches which can be transferred back to one's own classroom.

The first year will certainly be tough in terms of creating and sourcing teaching materials, but some of the above advice will hopefully make it less so. Ensuring that these resources are safely stored – electronically or in paper format – in folders for different topics or year groups in such a way as to be easily retrievable in future years is vital.

Accumulating resources over the years in this way hugely reduces a teacher's workload in terms of basic preparation, and liberates time to reflect upon *how* they are used, to make any necessary adaptations and to reflect upon what is successful and what is less so. Such a principle of consistently refining and improving what we use and what we do is part and parcel of the mastery approach which is fundamental to the excellent teacher's craft.

Managing technology

Any consideration of resources for learning and teaching in the 21st century would be incomplete without reference to the ever-expanding domain of technology. Anyone who is in any doubt that technology is an essential part of a modern teacher's toolkit, if they want to harness the attention and motivation of today's learners, would be well advised to watch the video clip on Teacher's Tube entitled *Pay Attention.*[6] This video reminds us that today's learners are above all digital learners who respond to technology because it feels entirely natural to them.

Familiarisation with, and use of, seemingly more arcane technological applications such as blogs, podcasts and wikis can have a significant impact on pupils' learning, and experimentation with these applications will be worth the investment of time on the teacher's part, since they are essentially simple and effective tools for communicating with pupils, enabling access to material and extending their learning beyond the confines of the classroom. However, the scope of this discussion permits only a consideration of the most widely available and most obviously useful tools for the beginning teacher.

Many, if not most, classrooms these days are equipped with a digital projector linked to a PC or laptop and, preferably, good quality speakers. The benefits of these simple but effective devices are manifold: they can provide an immediate link to the outside world through access to the internet and bring lessons to life through the use of striking images, a host of easily accessed audio material, video clips, graphics and animations. Furthermore, when such material is prepared in advance (including important text for notes or exemplification), the liberating effect on the teacher is substantial: we no longer need to spend a significant amount of time with our back to the class, writing on the board – which also aids classroom management – but can face our pupils, move around the room more freely and interact more readily with the class. The whole approach has thus become more active, lending relevance and interest and consequently increasing motivation and learning.

We have all, no doubt, heard of the dangers inherent in 'death by PowerPoint'. Quite possibly, we have suffered during a presentation where the speaker merely reads through slide upon slide of closely typed text, yet this easily available piece of software can be powerful and effective – if used imaginatively and discursively. This means avoiding the pitfalls of cluttered slides where pupils are bombarded with too much information – in the form of densely packed text projected all at once, and read to them in soporific tones. Rather, text can be animated so as to appear line by line or even word for word, enabling us to interact with pupils and to discuss the content before or as it appears on screen.

Moreover, slides can incorporate visuals, sound effects and hyperlinks to websites, video clips or associated documents. This can lead to a slicker, more professional and more modern delivery of lessons with text prepared in advance, and relevant files, clips and websites available at the mere click of a button.

PowerPoint presentations can also be shared with pupils for revision purposes, and absent pupils can be provided with a copy, thus facilitating their catching up with work missed. Slides can also be printed as handouts to guide pupils through the material as it is discussed in class (thus scaffolding the note-taking process for them), or used to review material at a later stage.

Interactive whiteboards (IWBs) are also becoming more prevalent in modern classrooms, but opinion is more divided on their benefits, particularly since some teachers in possession of one of these tools use it mainly or exclusively as a glorified projection screen. Such functionality can just as easily – and more cheaply – be obtained by means of a digital projector with conventional whiteboard or screen. The key distinction lies in the interactive nature of IWBs, and it may be that this lends itself more to some subjects than others.

The touch-sensitive screen of an IWB means that the functions of the computer desktop, projected on screen, can be controlled via the board using special pens or, with many board designs, a finger. This can be quicker and easier than using the keyboard or mouse, and pupils can be invited to come to the front and interact directly with the board. Other advantages include the ability to write over the top of existing programmes and displays (though this can also be achieved with a digital projector and normal whiteboard) and, more importantly, the opportunity to save anything which has been displayed as a key lesson point or for archive purposes. (For teachers with digital projectors only, this could be achieved by taking a digital photograph of the display or by allowing pupils to take photographs on their mobile phones!)

Finally, the IWB allows words, sections of text, graphs and shapes to be dragged around the board and manipulated. Such an approach can help pupils to grasp concepts such as the importance of word order in languages or the effect of an equation or a graph in mathematics, for example.

In short, although it would be fallacious to consider the use of ICT, or anything else for that matter, as an educational panacea, there is abundant evidence that, if used judiciously, it can significantly enhance learning. It should not be seen as an end in itself, however: 'Computers don't teach pupils; teachers do, and it's important for teachers to feel that technology is something that can support them, rather than control them. It's about introducing technology to address a particular need – and certainly not about purchasing the latest technology for its own sake.'[7]

One final word to the wise: any time we plan to use technology in a lesson, we should have an alternative up our sleeve. There will inevitably be lessons where problems arise and the technology simply will not work. For this reason, positive relationships with the ICT support staff and technicians are extremely important, and we should all ensure that we know the correct procedures for reporting problems so that they can be solved as quickly as possible.

Assessment for Learning

First-time teachers are also well advised to familiarise themselves with the approach referred to as Assessment for Learning and which is based on research at King's College, London, in the late 1990s. What follows below is a brief summary, and time spent reading the two original and concise publications, *Inside the Black Box* and *Working Inside the Black Box* will certainly pay dividends.[8] The former is more theoretical and the latter more practical in nature. In addition to these two seminal works, a range of related publications which are more subject-specific is now available.[9]

Assessment for Learning (AfL) is essentially good learning and teaching writ large. Much assessment in the past has been – and possibly still is in some classrooms – predominantly *of* learning, and has focused on assessment *of* performance in narrow, high-stakes tests: infrequent, isolated, special occasions over which teachers and learners often had little or no control. Some of this summative assessment is, of course, necessary; but the proponents of AfL would argue that if schools and teachers focus only on such assessment, this can have a harmful influence on teaching and learning, since it tends to promote rote or superficial learning rather than the development of understanding. Assessment *for* Learning, on the other hand, is informal and embedded in day-to-day practice, with different teachers assessing in their own diverse and individual styles. Such assessment aids learning and is known as *formative assessment*.

The AfL approach comprises four main strands: questioning, feedback, sharing success criteria and self and peer assessment. First, AfL encourages teachers to engineer effective class discussion through focusing on questioning techniques which cause thinking to take place and provide data which informs future teaching. We should plan, therefore, to include more open or 'rich' questions which cause higher-order thinking rather than only those which test simple recall.

These might include *why* or *how* questions; asking pupils: "Could you explain that a little more?"; "What made you think that?"; "X said this and Y said that – what do you think?"; "Could you build upon that?" We might also have groups working together to select, work out or evaluate the best answer to a question.

It may also prove advantageous to spend time with departmental colleagues preparing quality questions to promote thinking and discussion. It is certainly worth considering how we use questions to push pupils to the edge of their knowledge, since it is by so doing that we provide the necessary 'stretch' for them to learn. A recent article in the *Times Educational Supplement* quoted Professor John Hattie of Auckland University as follows: 'A teacher's job is not to make work easy. It is to make it difficult. If you are not challenged, you do not make mistakes. If you do not make mistakes, feedback is useless.'[10]

Another suggestion for improving our questioning is to allow a longer period of time to elapse before seeking answers to questions. The average 'wait time' in lessons observed by researchers from King's College, London, was 0.9 seconds! If this is increased to three seconds, for instance, we are likely to have longer, more thorough, better-quality answers with more pupils involved, particularly if the longer wait time is coupled with a 'no hands up' rule whereby pupils know that any one of them could be expected to answer the question posed. Such an approach means that no pupil can signal non-participation, although pupils need to know that it is acceptable, and sometimes useful, for them to be wrong – since an incorrect answer can still make thinking explicit and allow for the teacher or another pupil to intervene.

If we feel that 'no hands up' sessions may create anxiety among certain pupils, opportunities can be afforded for them to explore answers together first. The strategy known as 'think, pair, share' allows learners to come up with their own answer first, and to discuss this with a partner and then with others before a final response to the question is given.

Further strategies for involving *all* pupils in question and answer sessions include the use of mini whiteboards, true/false cards and cards labelled A, B, C, D for multiple choice questions. These can provide us with immediate evidence in terms of what every pupil has learned and allow us to plan our future teaching accordingly.

The second strand of AfL concerns feedback. Research studies have shown that good feedback improves performance in 60% of cases and it should both assess current achievement and indicate next steps. However, some thought has to be given to how we, as teachers, ensure that pupils take on board the feedback which we have provided – perhaps by specifying the minimum follow-up work expected by the next time that pupils' books are taken in.

Some ideas include a comment sheet[11] stuck in pupils' exercise books, or not providing complete solutions but indicating, for example, five questions which are wrong and having pupils find them – on their own or with a partner. Alternatively, we might place a dot in the margin each time we spot a mistake, and then expect pupils to find the error and correct it.

For our feedback to be effective, we may need to expend considerable time and care in terms of framing comments. Questions directed to the pupils in their exercise books are often an effective way of doing so, and these can establish a personal dialogue between teacher and pupil, leading to improved learning.

A more contentious view regarding feedback, based on research by Butler in 1988,[12] suggests that comments are more important than marks or scores. It is felt by some that pupils often ignore comments when marks are also given. Butler's research concludes that learning gains are greatest when only comments are included. Teachers, departments and schools must form their own view about this; but one possibility might be to provide only comments initially and then to ask pupils to think about which score they think their work deserves, based on clear marking criteria, before giving them the mark which we have awarded.

The third key strand of AfL involves sharing success criteria and making learning transparent. In the first instance, this might involve providing pupils with an overview of the work to be covered in any particular topic, term or school year. It also means sharing clear learning objectives with the pupils, planning lessons around the skills which we want pupils to learn and telling them explicitly how achievement can be demonstrated. Some of the best feedback which teachers provide takes the form of comments which make direct reference to success criteria that have been explained before a task is attempted.

Success criteria do not always need to be written lists, however. It can also be useful to show classes some exemplars of successful pupils' work and to discuss with them why pieces of work demonstrated are at a particular level or worth a particular mark. Teachers and departments might, therefore, over a number of years collect examples of A* performances at GCSE, for instance, and equivalent work from other year groups so that these can then be shown to subsequent pupils attempting similar tasks.

Finally, AfL encourages teachers to include more use of self and peer assessment. At the heart of this approach is the belief that the ability of pupils to direct their own learning is very important. Guy Claxton, Professor of Education at Bristol University, has referred to this as developing a pupil's 'nose for quality'.

It is suggested, then, that pupils need to be trained in self assessment so that they can understand the main purposes of their learning and what they need to do to achieve their goals. When such training has been promoted, pupils are able to say when and where they need help without a sense of failure and to work towards being in control of their own learning. In order for pupils to assess their own progress they require information about what they need to learn and how they will know they have been successful: *ie* a sound understanding of what constitutes good quality work.

Peer assessment is a means by which pupils share their understanding of 'quality' by assessing each other's work, again in relation to clear success criteria. It is argued that learning can be enriched, and motivation improved, when such opportunities are provided, particularly if pupils are expected to give reasons to justify their assessment of their own or another's work.

Conclusion

In conclusion, the key message for the beginning teacher should be that much of a teacher's craft can be learned, worked at and improved. Moreover, there is no such thing as the perfect teacher, and no-one has fully mastered the craft. However, through discussion with colleagues, a commitment to self-evaluation and reflection on our practice and a determination to rise to challenges one step at a time, we can all continuously become better teachers – the kind who make a real difference to pupils' lives.

References

[1] Mike Hughes, *Closing the Learning Gap*, Network Educational Press. 1999

[2] Michael Marland, *The Craft of the Classroom*, Heinemann. 2002

[3] Black, Harrison, Lee, Marshall, William, (2006) *Assessment for Learning. Putting IT into Practice*, OUP

[4] Michael Marland, *The Craft of the Classroom*, Heinemann, 2002

[5] www.tes.co.uk
http://tre.ngfl.gov.uk/
www.lgfl.net
www.bgfl.org/

[6] www.teachertube.com

[7] TES Essential Guide: *Technology and You*

[8] P Black & D Wiliam, *Inside the Black Box*, nferNelson, 1998 and P Black, C Harrison, C Lee, B Marshall & D Wiliam, *Working Inside the Black Box*, nferNelson, 2002

[9] www.gl-assessment.co.uk

[10] W Mansell quoting Professor J Hattie in *The answer to effective learning*, TES, 21st November 2008 www.tes.co.uk/article.aspx?storycode=6005411

[11] P Black, C Harrison, C Lee, B Marshall, D Wiliam, *Assessment for Learning. Putting IT into practice*, OUP, 2006, p47, and *Working Inside the Black Box*, nferNelson, 2002, p9

[12] R Butler, 'Enhancing and undermining intrinsic motivations: the effects of task-involving and ego-involving evaluation on interest and performance', *British Journal of Educational Psychology*, 58, 1998, pp1-14

Chapter 6

Achievement for all

Peter Hullah

Imagine a cartoon lesson 'starter' on the whiteboard. It shows two elderly Victorian archaeologists in the desert. One, with pipe in hand, contemplates a very small, pyramid-shaped rock which they have uncovered. The caption is: 'This could be the discovery of the century, depending of course how far down it goes.' We have looked into the future and know that the pyramid they have stumbled upon is huge. However when a searcher discovers only the top, to him, the rest is the great unknown.

So it is with teaching and learning. To the wise and experienced (and the two virtues are not always connected), the scope and breadth of the human brain is like a sponge with infinite capacity. To the NQT, the young brains in front of you are new, undiscovered territory and your main concern is to survive the heat of the day. How do we go deeper?

The archaeologist works with the smallest of brushes, carefully and lovingly, to unearth the grandest of discoveries. So the teacher works with every scrap of detail to build up a vast picture of learning. Start small and the picture will grow. Make the detail, the minute data, your friend.

'Starting small' means that you take time to know your students. First, know them by name and then show that you have learned about them. You have taken care to understand their background, their hopes and dreams. In files and on screens will be details of levels of progress, accounts of success, and records of failures. These are your building blocks for the lesson. Learn from the data, and value what you have learned. Then make plans. You know, as a good teacher, what level students should be working at, what level of achievement is expected of them and you have an ever-expanding tool kit to help your students make progress.

At the start of the year, explain what you expect of your class. This begins with explaining how you want them to line up outside the door, how you want them to enter the classroom and where you want each student to sit. You establish from the outset the language of the lesson. You outline in detail what you mean by 'paying attention'.

Teachers work very hard. Lessons are full to the brim with teacher preparation. They almost always show evidence of the midnight oil and often lesson plans have telltale red rings on them: evidence of Merlot-induced preparation. Yet a well-prepared lesson can miss the mark if there is no planning. You need to take into account the needs of each individual student and his or her journey from one learning milestone to another. That is planning. You can work very hard but if, when you stop for a moment, the class mentally goes on holiday, you may have prepared but not planned. It is said that in a good, well-planned lesson the teacher should do 20% of the work and the students 80%. Beware if it starts to feel like the other way round!

For an NQT, progress in a lesson must mean ensuring that it is the students who do the work of learning. This work will vary hugely in quantity and in style depending on ability, but without students working to learn, the best-prepared lesson does little apart from fill time.

Consider how a talented musician develops. First there is the spark of talent and then there is a lesson with an inspirational teacher who ignites that talent. However, the work of learning, of going deep down, takes place in the practice room. There, on your own, you try to master the art of a difficult phrase, going over and over it in fine detail until the notes become second nature. Therefore alongside the gifted teacher must come a support mechanism to ensure that the hours of practice are 'on task'. Students need to know that help is at hand when there is the temptation to give up.

There is a spark within every child, and it is the task of the teacher to ignite that spark. It is the task of the teacher to create a climate in a classroom where sparks ignite rather than fly. In this process you are not bounded by labels such as 'gifted and talented' or 'additional needs'. You are a treasure seeker who has one advantage over most treasure seekers. You know that treasure is there in front of you. To teach is to unlock talent. To teach well is to develop a mechanism, a series of systems for unearthing the treasure, layer by layer. It is more like the systematic work of *Time Team* than the lottery of *Britain's Got Talent!*

Returning to the detail of the lesson, your task as a teacher is to ensure that every student is on task all the time. This means that tasks are appropriate, understandable and challenging. No young person will engage with you in doing something which (s)he feels to be inappropriate. If (s)he does, it will be done unwillingly and therefore your words will fall on stony ground. No young person will engage in learning if (s)he does not understand 'why' this building block is essential. No students will come with you in learning if the task is not challenging. To select a task which is easy for the sake of a quiet life has short term gains (you usually survive until break) but you create no sense or patterns of learning. You establish no habit which is permanent in the student's mind.

Your lessons need to pass the test of being interesting and mind stretching, engaging and full of questions. The scientist is at an advantage here because the laboratory is a place of potential 'hands on wonder' where there is the possibility of an earth (or window!) shattering discovery every minute. For the historian or linguist or teacher of literature, envisage your classroom as a laboratory where discoveries can be made. Take your students to new places and be as excited as they become when they find pearls in unexpected places. If you think of your own days at school, the only lessons which remain in your mind are probably those taught by the teacher who had an infectious enthusiasm for some small detail. I have a passion for using the semicolon; this came from having lessons with a teacher who made me realise that accurate punctuation mattered, even though I have forgotten the precise detail of the lesson.

For an NQT, the heart of good practice is to keep students on task. That means *all students*, not merely those who like you for the moment (or those who appear to like you!). Visit other classrooms and watch teachers teach. Watch each student and ask yourself during the lesson: is every student on task and engaged? If so, where is praise? Is there more praise than criticism? The teacher needs to remember the proverb: 'It is when the sun shines that a man takes off his coat, not when the wind blows.'

If you count the number of times that students are on task when somebody else is teaching, you will find that you start counting instinctively during your own lessons. You will, out of habit, include boys as well as girls (or vice versa): you will, out of habit, know who the slow learner is. Then you will find ways of taking that child forward: you will know that the mind of the bright-eyed brain box will need to be nourished and fed with questions which lead to questions. When such children are on task, time will fly by and you will know, for a fleeting moment, why you decided to come into teaching.

The good teacher uses praise with surgical skill. Reinforce good behaviour, and bad behaviour will begin to evaporate. When you praise someone, say "well done". But don't stop there. Say "well done, Lizzie" or "Mike". But don't stop there. Say "well done Lizzie for that answer, which made us all think. You really understand why the battle was lost but the war was won".

The NQT starting out on a teaching career is beginning a journey. Look at the *Opening Minds* material produced by the Royal Society of Arts and you will see the research which has helped to develop an understanding of learning competencies. At whatever level you are teaching, you should be aware of those competencies; aware of how the mind works and aware, simply, of how we learn. Talk to others about this; share your insights into how your classes are learning and you will be an inspiration to others. More than that, you will become inspirational.

Life does not end when you graduate or qualify: rather it begins. Every NQT should have a mentor and an agreed programme of continuing professional development, established by the school and allowing time for professional conversations. Your mentor will coach and guide you into thinking differently. In the very early days of teaching, keep a diary of what has worked in your teaching and ask for feedback. Be courageous and encourage others to come and see you teach. Ask them to bring with them a clicker and to tell you how many students were on task in a ten-minute period of the lesson. Ask their opinion about whether you included the slow learner or only the 'professor'.

Very few people come into teaching because it is a job. At some stage in your career something stirred and you felt a sense that you wanted to teach. It is a kind of 'calling': a vocation to make the world a better place by investing in the next generation. By teaching, you are building the future and the greatest sense of achievement comes when you feel that through your efforts the future is in safe hands. Because of what you are doing in small ways in the classroom, you have diminished the possibility that the weak go to the wall. You have opened minds, unlocked and discovered that all have a distinctive spark and that there is a place and a purpose for everyone in shaping the future.

Your mark book will show a clear record of individual progress, in forensic detail. You will be able to show evidence of progress taking place and you will have asked question after question about how learning is having an effect on smaller and smaller groups of students. You will, with practice, be able to say more than "That was a good lesson". You will know from evidence that Roshana, who is not good at maths, had made a real leap forward; that Danny, who maybe is in a set too low, has done an amazing assignment on the Hubble telescope which you want to send to the astronauts; that Danielle has discovered she wants to be a vet and is prepared to work to qualify; and that Peter has discovered the beauty and the poetry of a well-used semicolon.

To work at a good school is to know first hand that there is more to life than examinations grades. The tests are the beginning. However they are only the first stage, the hurdles over which we jump so that we have access to wider horizons. It will be the values which you hold about your life which will guide your students into the future when memories of tests fade. The role of the teacher and the school community is to communicate a set of lasting values in explicit and implicit ways. You must know what your school 'stands for'. You must know what 'key values' underpin the leadership. Then you must live those values in every lesson and demonstrate that they matter.

Your priorities will become the priorities of your students and, if it matters to you, it will matter for them also. If you hold every action as being for 'The Best in Everyone', as we do in the Academy in which I work, then little by little you will play your part in shaping character, in forming lives which are open to learning. Some of the wisest words ever said are: 'You never know the effect you have on others.' Every conversation, every lesson, every professional relationship and every mark has the potential for growth and change for an individual student in ways we may never realise. That is one of the most exciting and challenging aspects of teaching. Believe in your students and they will come to believe in their ability to live their dreams.

As an NQT you bring freshness to the profession which we should value and treasure. The excitement is that the effect and impact of your teaching and learning, like the tip of that undiscovered pyramid, may go down much further than you imagine.

Chapter 7

Extra and co-curricular opportunities

Brenda Despontin

There was little hesitation when I asked my son, Jonathan, what advice he would offer to other NQTs. Only recently in possession of a GTP certificate himself, he spoke with the conviction of one who knows: "For heaven's sake, don't say yes to everything at the start. You won't be able to keep up with all the extras you'll be asked to run or join, and it's really important to still have a life outside the job, especially in a boarding school."

It is a sad indictment of our training system for teachers that so many leave the profession after just a year or two in the classroom. Some no doubt have realised that the rather artificial world of school is not for them, and they probably ought not to have trained in the first place, but others have simply been exhausted by the relentless routines, constant battles with disaffected students and the interminable, mindless paperwork.

Ironically, involvement in extracurricular activities with students, for all the additional time commitment that they imply, can nevertheless provide a whole new dimension to working in a school and can offer a positive context for the less satisfying demands of the job. Suddenly those difficult Year 9 boys are 'your' footie team; that reticent Year 4 child with English as a second language has an exquisite singing voice and leads the choir; the sullen girl with black lipstick in Year 10 unexpectedly and quite magically takes the lead and lifts everyone's spirits on a difficult, very damp Duke of Edinburgh's Award scheme expedition.

Involvement with students in activities like these outside the classroom is an absolute must for newcomers to the teaching profession. The ease with which things subsequently proceed to develop back in the classroom is a regular experience for new teachers. Some form of bonding has occurred with 'sir' or 'miss', some rite of passage, which makes the core business of their teaching and learning more palatable, and classroom management much easier.

I still recall my own experiences with a really difficult class and in particular the acned, tattooed, shaven-headed Darren whose *raison d'être* was to make as much mischief in school as was humanly possible between the hours of nine and four. As a new teacher I was easy pickings, and I realised that the text books and tutorials of the PGCE had not quite covered how to react to Darren's frequent, defiant Anglo-Saxon expletives.

The school's drama festival required us to enter a play as a form. Whatever could I ask Darren to do? He had already dismissed the whole idea anyway with his perfected sneer – and no one in the form really wanted him involved. "He'll spoil it, miss" said one, but well out of Darren's earshot, of course. The play's success rested on the curtains being closed at just the right moment at its end. *Faute de mieux*, Darren had a job! I told him it was *the* most important part of the play, and that he had to simultaneously operate a tape recorded gunshot at that precise moment of the curtains closing.

How did this end? Well, said play was a success and won the festival prize. As for Darren, he rose to the challenge with aplomb and never gave me a minute's trouble ever again. Now, I'd like to say this was planned behaviour management based on some pedagogical theory, but actually I was still stumbling my way through the early days in the job, and it was just chance – but it worked. I have never forgotten the lesson it taught me, namely that extracurricular opportunities enable *all* children to discover what often eludes them elsewhere, at home and in the classroom.

Such occasions focus on what children 'can do'; they give them a chance to shine in a non-judgemental setting and often make them feel special. Holding those curtain chords made Darren powerful in a positive way: people depended on him, they trusted him, and he delivered. The praise he got from his peers afterwards was probably the first he had ever received.

Unlike so many other careers, teaching offers a unique chance to share with young minds not just the knowledge and skills we have, or the passion for a particular discipline, but also what makes us who we are as individuals – our hobbies and interests beyond the curriculum and outside the confines of the job. We have a chance to pass on to others what someone once passed to us, whether it was the English teacher who ran an 'Appreciation of Art' club, or the physics master who ran the school cricket for 20 years.

But NQTs beware! Each September, the staffroom elders wait in anticipation of the shiny new arrivals: with just a single café latte in a decent mug together with the promise of a locker above knee height, they can lure an unexpected apprentice into running clubs and teams which no one has wanted to tackle for some time.

By all means get involved, but beware the poisoned chalices collecting bacteria on the staff room draining board! Be sure to ask how much time will be required, why no one is currently involved, and how the funding operates for that activity. New to the school and the career, you must never feel guilty when you give yourself time to relax, to enjoy 'downtime' with friends and family and to *stop* thinking of school. The key, as my son points out, is to get the balance right.

There are many maintained schools with excellent extracurricular programmes and an army of dedicated staff delivering the best they can for some often very deprived children. We read of government-backed initiatives to increase the CCF opportunities for example, or to take dance and drama professionals into inner city schools.

But it is fair to say that the range and scope of activities outside and beyond the curriculum is a real strength in the independent sector. Boarding and day schools alike will boast a staggering range of choice in sport, from the traditional rugby, hockey, netball, cricket and lacrosse to the more exotic – fencing, archery and water polo. The chance to be part of a team, and to represent the school, the county and even the country, be it in rowing, equestrian events, as lacrosse champions or gymnasts, is invaluable in the development of character. Such talents can lead to international recognition and they most definitely influence university offers.

Opportunities are equally plentiful in the performing arts, where music of all styles, and drama for all ages and ability levels, are customer expectations. Not only that, but these activities often lead to overseas tours or external competitions, or to world-famous events such as the Edinburgh Festival.

Of particular value are the many examples of outdoor pursuits. In an age where we limit the exposure to risk, it is important to give students a chance to test their own resilience, and many teachers have considered an involvement in a World Challenge expedition, or the CCF or the Duke of Edinburgh's Award scheme as being part of their own professional development: a real learning opportunity for them as well as for their pupils. If we aim to challenge and inspire young minds, it matters that we include ourselves in that ambition, and NQTs will find many ways in which their involvement is sought and valued.

Good independent schools offer junior and senior debating clubs, public speaking, charities committees, school newspapers, and a kaleidoscope of clubs for enthusiasts (students and staff) who harbour a passion for everything from chess to film, flower arranging to Sudoku. But with some rehearsals or fitness training happening before school starts, lunchtimes packed with activities, and evening and weekend programmes full to capacity, a new teacher can quickly be swamped with requests, and may find it difficult to refuse senior colleagues or disappoint persuasive students.

Told by the Head on appointment that you'll get out of the post what you put in, and keen to build the CV, NQTs fear their refusal will convey the wrong message. Best advice (from my son again) is to talk this through early in the year, with the mentor or head of department, and to agree on a sensible extracurricular spread of activities, some employing existing interests and skills but some which provide invaluable professional development too, such as helping to organise a trip overseas.

Boarding schools often offer free accommodation to resident house tutors: a real attraction for cash-strapped NQTs still burdened with student debt. However, there are duties and extracurricular demands built into that deal, in addition to the classroom teaching. If you agree to run a team, the time-off residential duties might disappear as you arrange another practice or accompany the team to an away fixture. Some will relish that extra commitment, having benefited themselves as students from such opportunities, and as teachers they will quickly see the benefits of knowing the students better.

But a boarding environment, for all its many advantages, rewards and career satisfaction, can be a bubble which takes over your life. Contacts met regularly outside that somewhat rarefied, enclosed world will make a new teacher a more balanced individual. If possible, therefore, keep your old college contacts, and nurture friendships beyond the school gates with those from other professions: conversations will thus not be entirely about school, and there is undoubtedly an advantage in hearing about the pitfalls in other careers when it seems you are in the worst one! Remember, you will be watching your students on the ski slopes, or showing them the Uffizi Gallery when your friends are deskbound in the City, or working round the clock in A&E.

There are some caveats which it is important to observe when undertaking extracurricular responsibilities. Read carefully the school handbook on health and safety to be sure you comply. Complete and submit risk assessment forms as required for all trips and visits and do your homework well in advance if you are staying somewhere overnight. Check any details with experienced staff if you have a doubt about them, and do not believe all that the students tell you about what was permitted on previous trips!

Be clear on the policy about alcohol, and on allowing students to wander off unsupervised. Establish, before you accompany any trip, exactly what is expected of you: as an NQT, there is much to learn from being part of a successful, well-managed tour or expedition, but it should not be you who is left on late duty every night.

If you are running sports teams, then, in a litigious world, it is wise to acquire coaching qualifications and first aid training to underpin your enthusiasm. They are useful additions to the CV anyway, and there are many who believe it a sensible precaution to join a union, through which legal cover is provided.

It is worth remembering too that student enthusiasm is an unreliable beast: your war games club might have attracted 20 committed regulars in the dark, rainy days of November, but when the May blossoms and the cricket whites are brought out from hibernation, you must not be disappointed by the fact that only two stalwarts remain. 'Twas ever thus, and you might decide to pack away the combatants for the season and give everyone a break. They may well return to it all refreshed and enthusiastic, once the days begin to draw in again.

As a final caveat, remember that you will be tested as an NQT: students will want to know where the parameters are; to know what is acceptable to you; whether you are on the side of the students or the teachers. You will need to act according to the school culture and rules, but think it all through beforehand.

What will you do when your sportsmen swear in your earshot? What will you do when the Year 10 couple start getting physical in the coach on the way home from that theatre trip? What will you do when a student on your school newspaper team submits a highly controversial piece: well-written, but critical of the school management? What might have been an excellent piece for the university rag you once edited could be wholly inappropriate at your school.

Remember: you *will* occasionally get it wrong at the beginning, but preparation and forethought help limit those disasters, along with a willingness to be open and yes, at times, humble with your mentor. Becoming a good teacher is a lifelong journey and being an NQT is a very early first step.

On a recent car journey, my willing NQT interviewee expanded further on his advice to the next cohort new to the profession: "Be a sponge," he said. "Observe as often as you can – with anyone who's willing, in whatever discipline. You'll learn so much every time, acquiring skills everywhere, and you can then incorporate them into your own style. Get involved in school life, but set attainable goals for yourself: I tried to achieve too much at the start and had no idea I'd get so tired. Even with both parents in the profession, I had not appreciated the intensity and the pace until I did the job myself – teaching three new courses with exam classes, with boarding duties and my teams to coach, I need some downtime too. But the best advice is, relish all the challenges and remember to enjoy it! You're lucky to be in the best job there is."

(With thanks to Jonathan, who is finally doing what I always knew he would!)

76

Chapter 8

The effective use of time

Nigel Richardson

Whether you use an internet search engine or an old-fashioned book of quotations, wise one-liners about Time are easy to find. The first Queen Elizabeth once said that she would: "Give all my possessions for a moment of time." Benjamin Franklin coined the phrase: "Time is money". He also told us: "Then do not squander time, for that's the stuff that life is made of."

Napoleon told people to: "Ask of me anything but my time." The famous novelist W H Auden tells us not to be deceived by time, because we cannot conquer it. President John F Kennedy declared that: "We must use time as a tool, not as a couch." And, according to Shakespeare, Richard II admitted that he: "Wasted time and now doth time waste me."

Just over half a century ago, Professor C Northcote Parkinson devised the celebrated Parkinson's Law: 'Work expands so as to fill the time available for its completion.' General recognition of this fact is shown in the proverbial phrase: "It is the busiest man who has time to spare."

We owe a related idea to him, too: that 'The Law of Triviality… briefly stated means that the time [in meetings] spent on any item of the agenda will be in inverse proportion to the sum of money involved'. As you get established in your school, and as meetings come and go, you will probably find that his words have more than a ring of truth about them.

As other writers in this volume will tell you, any new job puts particular demands on someone in their first year, and teaching is certainly no exception. When interviewing potential teachers for their first job, and questioning them about the skills and interests that they might be able to bring to my school, I was inclined to be wary not only of those who appeared to offer too little, but also of those who promised to do *too much* in their first year.

I tried to assess their ability to pace themselves. As I did so, my eyes sometimes strayed to the huge row of A4 folders on my study bookshelves: teaching notes accumulated over 35 years or so. They were an instantly available resource, but I was all too aware that it takes time to build them up. By contrast, in the first year (or two, or three) you are teaching everything for the first time, so there are big demands in terms of lesson preparation – as well as the demands arising from all those extracurricular activities which you volunteered to take part in at your interview.

It is also fair to say that teaching tends to attract people who are above-averagely conscientious – occasionally to the point of being obsessive. Moreover, as a profession we are often rather good at creating new ideas for the curriculum and other activities (and the work for ourselves which goes with them), but rather less skilled at killing off an idea or scheme which has passed its sell-by date and which the new scheme is designed to replace.

Meanwhile, in recent years there have been technological and social developments which add to our potential workload. Cheaper and more numerous telephones and more sophisticated switchboards in schools make teachers more accessible than they once were. Email has transformed our lives in our dealings both with parents and our pupils – for worse as well as better. In boarding schools, parents visit their children far more frequently than previous generations did. There are many more families in both boarding and day schools in which both parents work – sometimes in order to afford our fees.

Above all, many parents *worry* – and it often seems that there is plenty potentially for them to worry about. The mass media has huge coverage of educational issues – exam performance; SATs; complex conditions such as dyslexia, dyspraxia, dyscalculia, ADHD (Attention Deficit Hyperactivity Disorder) and SAD (Seasonal Affective Disorder). Moreover, the lifestyle supplements in newspapers are full of lurid descriptions of troubled parenting and difficult teenagers, including every conceivable issue from emotional intelligence and issues of identity or sexuality, to the effect of drugs or the pros and cons of the gap-year.

For every parent who complains about something, there are probably at least two who just need simple reassurance from their child's teachers.

Closer and regular contact between teacher and parent is highly beneficial in lots of ways, but all those contacts and meetings take time. This communication culture also represents a huge change: it is sometimes hard to realise that many schools had no parents' evenings *at all*, even a few decades ago. I write from the experience of having worked in one.

How, then, do we find ways of fitting in all the demands being made on us? Being able to manage time effectively as an NQT is highly important, and good organisational skills can make a huge difference, not only to the amount of ground that you cover, but also to the quality of your life. Buildings, plant, machinery and books are all important resources and we plan and budget for them. But time is an equally vital resource, and one which all too often goes unrecognised as such, and which, as a result, goes unplanned and unbudgeted for.

Many of us think of work too much in terms of hours done, and too little in terms of effectiveness and results achieved. This can be the case whether we are considering what we ourselves have to do this week or whether we are advising our exam candidates about how to do their holiday revision. Some of us give advice freely, yet we do not always act on that advice ourselves.

The following suggestions may help, even if some of them seem obvious. Many people still ignore them – yet once you have learned how to work effectively on the tasks which have to be done, it will become easier to sort out and plan the tasks themselves.

First: some general principles. If you didn't get to know these as a sixth former or university student, now is the time.

Eat and drink moderately and exercise regularly. Make sure that your working conditions are comfortable, but not too much so (although I realise that at school one's personal work space can be very limited). Sufficient heat is important; light needs to be properly distributed. Many people find it better to work with a window to one side, rather than in front. Make sure there is a good fresh air supply. Try to avoid too much noise, either from traffic or background music.

Try to work at the times of day when you know you are at your best mentally. If you are one of the 40% who are 'morning people', it is no use trying to burn the midnight oil every night. Far better to get up earlier, perhaps going into school before the morning traffic really builds up. Use your prime working time to do those tasks that demand the most mental effort. Preparing new lessons is one example of this; going through old files to throw things away can be left until a time when your brain is less alert. (Maybe marking falls somewhere between the two.)

Try not to concentrate for very long periods without a break. Most experts advise five to ten minutes per hour of complete mental and physical relaxation. If you have to digest complicated new information, don't just sit and stare at printed pages hour after hour.

Make notes which will jog the memory later. Write down key theme words. Develop your own 'shorthand' code words. Think of as many ways as possible of memorising information. Visualising things is all-important. Mnemonics (making words out of the first letters of a list of names) and word associations can be a great help.

Whether writing or typing up notes, make sure that they are effectively laid out. Use headings wherever possible. Number your points. Indent subpoints well to the right of the margin. Space things out and make sure that you do not end up with a piece of paper on which every line is filled up right across the page. Use coloured underlinings and highlighter pens, but not too much, or you will end up with a beautiful but illegible page of many colours.

Consider taking a course in rapid reading, if you think you need one. Teach yourself to write so that others can read it. Teach yourself to type – if you haven't already. For many years it was said that far fewer British executives (compared with those abroad) learned the art of touch-typing properly, yet it saves time and increases accuracy. Some schools will give you assistance in acquiring a laptop; others may loan out or even give away PCs for which the school no longer has any use.

And then there are the emails: we all get far too many of them. Try to deal with them regularly, rather than letting them accumulate – and seek to develop the art of spotting which ones (especially from parents and colleagues) need an immediate answer and which do not. Don't be afraid to use a holding reply for those of the latter type.

Those copied to you (as opposed to those sent to you personally) do not usually require a reply at all. When writing to others, resist the temptation to spray copies of the emails you send to all and sundry; they are fighting time pressures, too. Heads, just like those at the top of other organisations, quickly learn to spot people who over-copy things in an attempt to show how hard they work!

Above all, do one thing at a time whenever possible. Keep your desk tidy and organised. Diary management will also help you, and the section which follows applies both to traditional ways of doing things (*eg* the written diary, Filofax *etc*) and to those who prefer the electronic personal organiser.

Get into one single place all the information about your teaching timetable, the school calendar, the times of your meetings with people and a list of your tasks and deadlines (*eg* report writing). This will give you a comprehensive map of the day and week ahead – or even longer. You may choose to combine it with your mark-book or marking records. If you choose to operate from a traditional desk diary, acquire one which runs from September to August rather than January to December. Your school may well place a central order for these each year.

As you slowly fill up your diary, try to make sure that there is a little slack time built into each day to allow for the unforeseen or to give you a break. Consult it each morning – for several reasons: to check what must be done today; to see what was left undone yesterday; and to see what is listed under tomorrow which might well be done today if time unexpectedly allows. Carry a small notebook at all times to jot down tasks and appointments which arise when you don't have your diary or organiser with you. Transfer these into the diary every day.

From week-to-week, make lists of tasks which need to be done within an approximate time span rather than by an exact deadline – next year's match arrangements, next term's speaker bookings, *etc*. Take a broader look at the diary at the start of each week. Spot likely pressure points in advance and take action to spread the workload out around them.

The same principles can be applied to a longer period of time. It will not take long each summer to transfer regularly recurring items from one year's diary to the next. This is an excellent way of charting the year ahead and of making sure that routine tasks do not get forgotten next year.

Diaries can also be useful retrospective tools as well as planning ones. Look back at the week just ended on, say, Monday mornings. Note where the last week's main pressure points were, and learn from experience; if Wednesday is always a heavy teaching day, try to compensate by moving some tasks to Tuesday in the week ahead.

Apply the same principles termly and annually. Does exam setting need more time than you gave it this term? Just occasionally, conduct a more detailed review: divide the day just past into 15- or 30-minute slots and work out exactly what you did in them. Then allocate an effectiveness rating to each – say, one for very useful and five for a complete waste of time. What proportion of your time was spent on grade one activities?

You can also work out how much time in the week has been spent on each activity: study/lesson preparation; marking; teaching; games; extracurricular activities; meetings and interviews; travelling; thinking; relaxation and sleeping. Don't underestimate the importance of the last three!

There are dangers in becoming a complete time fanatic, as described by a Cambridge historian, Professor Jonathan Steinberg:

> 'The unexpected caller, pleasant or unpleasant, disturbs the pattern of your time. That time is already allotted. Hence there is no time to help somebody who needs it, to relax and enjoy a chat on the street.
>
> Enjoyment is always for after when all the jobs with deadlines, the letters to be answered, the calls to be made, have been despatched. But that time never comes. There are always more letters, deadlines, jobs and so life gets postponed until an indefinite after – until it is too late. A hamster on a treadmill has about the same sort of freedom.'

Using time effectively should always be an ambition but it should never become an obsession.

None of us can do all that we would like to, so we must draw up priorities. Once the mechanics of charting and reviewing time have been worked out, future priorities can be analysed more effectively. Ask yourself a few searching questions: Do I need to create more *thinking* time? Are routine tasks either getting crowded out or eating too much into *creative* time? Could I eliminate some of the interruptions to my work each day? Am I allowing enough time to cope with the unexpected? Have I created enough margins, both in my job and in my private life, to prevent me from constantly being rushed and fraught? Am I getting enough rest and relaxation to make my work effective?

You also need some actions to solve the issues arising from these questions. These might include making a list of daily 'to-dos'. Try to compile it at the same time each day, so that you establish a routine. List the tasks and give them priority classification, say:

A - must be done today;
B - ideally would be done today;
C - must be done sometime, but could be tomorrow or later;
D - would be done ideally some time, but ultimately not essential.

Then label the most urgent A1, followed by A2, B1 and so on.

Make sure that you have one consolidated list rather than a collection of scraps of paper. Do the A tasks first: *always*. If you find you have a spare ten minutes here and there, don't fill it with a C task, but do part of an A task instead – otherwise the A tasks will never get done. The A tasks which look overwhelmingly large can often be subdivided into ten-minute sessions.

Never postpone tasks merely because they are unpleasant. They will nag away in your subconscious and cause needless stress. Better to have something pleasant to look forward to. Stick to deadlines wherever possible. Try to anticipate how long each task will take; most people consistently underestimate, so add 20% for good measure. Unrealistic goals lead to unmet deadlines which in turn can cause depression and tiredness. Allow margins for the unexpected. Ask yourself frequently: "What is the best use of my time right now?"

Some years ago, a management training film showed a stressed executive dismissing the suggestion that he should analyse his actions with the words: "Who's got time to think about time? I've got too much to think about already." This chapter has tried to show that time is one of the most important things to think about.

Natural energy and stamina are often said to be the two ingredients of dynamism in people. They are certainly a great help – but to some extent you can make up for lack of them by an intelligent use of time and by pacing yourself. Many of these techniques take time to learn; some come only with experience. But it is worth persevering.

If you master your time, you master your life.

Chapter 9

Communication with parents

Peter de Voil

There are different categories of parents. There are the sympathetic parents who value education, who have thought long and hard about the school and who, in some cases, may have worked hard to save up enough money to pay the school fees, often with the help of grandparents, by moving to a smaller house or going without a new car or expensive holidays. These parents are on your side; they may even help with social functions, career seminars or with offers of accommodation for exchange pupils, *etc.* They are usually reasonable people.

Then there are the busy, wealthy parents who have recently bought a new house, a new SUV, and a place at a new school – yours. They may have heard about your school from friends, from newspaper articles (league tables?) or their child's previous school – or they may not have done much research beyond realising that the school is sufficiently 'posh' or just conveniently situated for them. These parents may be demanding and unreasonable.

There is another important category too: the divorced or one-parent family, where the anxiety level about a child's progress and welfare may often be quite high. These parents may rely on the school to provide a degree of stability and security which is lacking at home. Sometimes they can feel insecure and uncertain – even guilty – as to whether, or how, their break-up may have affected their children; occasionally they may blame them too. A proportion of them may displace these feelings onto the school in the way in which they perceive its performance. They can be demanding in a different way.

However, all parents have to be dealt with even-handedly: they are our customers, they pay our salaries, and they have a choice of others schools if we fail to meet their expectations. Satisfied parents are also our best advertisement as they recommend the school to friends and neighbours. A strong partnership with parents is essential, and good relationships and good communication with parents should be the norm.

Almost all parents will expect instant access to the school, to be able to communicate with the school by email or phone. They will expect a prompt response – from the teaching staff as well as the Head. However, they often forget that teachers spend most of their day in the classroom, out on the games field or elsewhere, and that they are not sitting in front of a computer, ready to respond to the arrival of every email within minutes.

It is likely that school's handbook for parents will set out the correct channels of communication: for example, via the subject teacher, form tutor or housemaster in the first instance, depending on the nature of the communication, then the head of year or head of department if a problem remains unresolved. If parents do request a meeting with you, insist they make an appointment, ask them what the issue is and brief yourself carefully by reading the child's file beforehand and consulting other staff if necessary.

If the issue is likely to be a difficult one, it is wise to have someone else with you: your head of department or even the Head. In your first year, it is good practice not to take meetings alone, and in some schools it will be policy for *all* staff to conduct parental meetings with a colleague present. One of you should take notes of the meeting.

If it is a complaint, it may well have come from the child and will sometimes be inaccurate, exaggerated or unjustified. You may have spoken firmly or critically to the child, because of inattention in class, failure to have the right books, arriving late for the lesson, or not handing in homework on time, *etc.* The pupil has telephoned, or complained at home, that he or she has been unfairly treated.

Handled firmly but sensitively, a meeting can turn out very successfully, with parents going away thinking that you have listened to their concerns or complaints and in most cases explained what really happened and put the matter straight. You should not be aggressive to parents or unduly defensive, but you must not allow yourself to be bullied by them.

More difficult is the demand that a child change classes to be taught by another teacher on the grounds that you (or one of your colleagues) are incompetent, unfair, too strict, too lax, are incomprehensible, too slow or too fast, or a combination of these! This may have arisen out of a child's need to defend poor results or a critical report at home by blaming the teacher; or you may be setting high standards that the child cannot or will not reach.

It is also possible that at one end of the success/failure spectrum the child is having genuine difficulties or, at the other, that (s)he is not being stretched, and if you know this, you can take appropriate steps to remedy it. However, it may be that the child is not flourishing in your class and, with your approval and that of a higher authority, the child could move to another class and another teacher. However, a move may not be possible for timetabling reasons or because of limits on the size of classes, and you won't want to set a precedent, so the usual reaction must be to say "no". Never be pushed into making a promise that you can't deliver, or which needs to be referred to people up the school's chain of command.

The phone call can be the biggest menace, because if a parent phones you, it is difficult to avoid taking the call. If the parent is merely sending you some information about a child's absence or illness, or asking a question about homework, there is no problem, but if it is a complaint you need to be much more careful, say that you will look into it and get back to the caller. Not to respond promptly will merely increase that parent's anxiety, frustration or anger.

I can remember as a housemaster in the early days of mobile phones receiving a call in mid-morning from an irate mother claiming that her daughter had just been assaulted by her biology teacher and asking what was I going to do about it. I normally try not to run, but I did so on this occasion, with images of police, ambulances and a hostile press swirling round in my head.

It transpired that the hapless teacher (now a Head in his own school) had demanded some overdue homework by that afternoon, and to emphasise the last three words had poked the girl in the chest with his finger three times – not a wise move. It was some time ago: in those days, fortunately, a telephoned apology from me, a letter of apology from him and an additional sentence in the staff handbook ended the matter. Nowadays such a response might lead to far more serious, formal disciplinary action. Times, and expectations, have changed.

Some say that day schools suffer most from such knee-jerk responses, but I can also remember receiving regular angry phone calls from a mother in Hong Kong, claiming that the school nurse did not like her son and was not giving him the proper treatment for his (many) so-called ailments. Knowing a little about this mother and realising that she was probably ringing at the same time each evening, I plucked up courage to ask her to ring before, rather than after, her gin and tonic – and it worked!

So how is it best to deal with emails? It is important to find time to respond to them quickly. You need to try to check your emails more than once a day. I usually do this before school starts, at lunchtime and before I leave after school. While email communication is quick and convenient, the formal exchange of letters that we were used to in the past could be time-consuming but it enabled us to make careful enquiries and reflect on our answer.

Now there is a temptation to dash off a reply sooner rather than later to clear the screen and to move on. This can be a mistake. However, don't be afraid to send a non-committal, holding reply: some form of instant acknowledgement, thanking the sender for his or her email and saying that you will look into the matter and reply in due course, is essential. This will give you time to look at the child's file, and to consult those who may need to be consulted, including your line manager or a member of the senior management team, if school policy is involved.

What about the angry, provocative or downright rude email, which we all get from time to time? It is tempting to send a brilliantly witty or cutting response – don't! It will only make you feel good until you get the reply. Sleep on it, and then carefully and systematically deal with each point in a calm, factual, non-inflammatory manner. Discuss it with your line manager or the Head, who may wish to take the matter out of your hands and deal with it personally. Some schools have a clause in the parental contract that if a parent behaves unreasonably, he or she can be asked to withdraw the child from the school.

It is often a good idea to start your considered reply with an apology, not necessarily for a mistake you have made or an ill-judged action that you are alleged to have carried out (unless this is the case, when an apology is of course justified), but simply for the fact that the correspondent has felt it necessary to write in and complain. This can be a good tactic: such replies have a disarming effect. You should probably end your reply with a comment such as: 'I hope I have managed to answer your complaint/allay your fears/reassure you.' Or you could then suggest a meeting if the correspondent thinks that the problem has not been resolved to his/her satisfaction.

Schools rely increasingly on their ICT systems. You should know how to file email correspondence electronically so that it can be retrieved easily; it is wise to copy all exchanges of email with parents and place those copies on the pupil's file. Notes of telephone conversations should also be taken, dated and kept in the same way. If a parental complaint develops into a serious dispute, a written record of who said what and when may be essential.

Some schools publish school email addresses for parents and urge them to contact individual teachers directly, and you can use the system to your own advantage, sending out parental updates, reminders and small news items – or to chase them for the forgotten forms which have fallen victim to the black hole which is (all too often) the student school bag! Some teachers have their own weblogs and are happy for pupils to communicate with them directly, but it should not be school policy to give out teachers' private email addresses, at least not without their permission.

You may well ask your pupils for their emails so that you can send them reminders, revisions tips, relevant notes, details of sources of information and references for their essays, *etc*, and they can send you their homework or queries about work you have set. In all cases, follow the school's policy on electronic communication, and avoid the informality which email sometimes seems to encourage.

What about confidentiality? We all need to be aware that clever, determined pupils seem able to hack into email systems and to access correspondence which can then be circulated among pupils or even forwarded to a newspaper. Unless you are sure that your system is 100% secure, it is wise not to entrust anything confidential or sensitive to email, and also to refrain from making any derogatory comments that could be embarrassing to you or to others if published. *The Independent* once put this very succinctly: 'Never put in an email something you wouldn't want your boss, your aunt, a lawyer or *The Independent* to see.'

Emails can also be copied by mistake to others. I once sent a detailed analysis of a pupil with behavioural problems to my cousin in New Zealand, who used to run the Milk Marketing Board there; and I recall a fellow-housemaster who once wrote to a parent agreeing that one of his colleagues was worse than useless: unfortunately he sent it to the colleague rather than the parent...

There is also the story of the Head of a distinguished school sending his application for the Headship of an even more distinguished school to his deputy by mistake! Having said that, it is of course good practice to keep other members of staff informed, especially if you are a form tutor or housemaster, by passing on news about pupils' absences, illnesses, achievements, *etc* by email, but if the information is sensitive, check with the person concerned that you can do this.

Writing reports also needs careful attention. For most parents these are important documents, which will be studied very carefully at home, shared with grandparents and kept on file. These days, parents expect a brief summary of what has been taught, an analysis of performance and progress, a judgement, and advice on what needs to be done in future. They are also of course a report on the teacher and thus on your teaching!

Once again be honest, but even if your assessment is largely negative or pessimistic, *always* try to find something positive to say – and avoid flippant or sarcastic remarks. I can remember remarks like 'He is so laid back that he is almost horizontal' being returned to be rewritten, or the remark 'He is a bear of little brain' getting through and causing parents great distress.

As a Head, I have insisted that reports suggesting that a pupil is a waste of time and space must be rewritten. And if you claim that a pupil repeatedly arrives late for your lessons or fails to hand in homework, the parents may with some justification ask why you are allowing this to happen and what are you doing about it! Parents also get upset if the end-of-term report reveals for the first time that a pupil is behaving or performing badly; they will expect to have been notified about this earlier in the term.

Parents' meetings are equally important, and for many it will be the only time they meet you. This is where you display your professionalism. Some parents may also be teachers themselves, or experts in your own subject. Time is usually quite short, and parents will go away with a strong impression – for better or worse. They may be nervous, particularly if their child is struggling in your subject, so again be realistic but give them hope! Remember that your role is pastoral as well as academic. You must be well prepared: make sure you know each pupil's strengths and weaknesses, and make sure you talk about the right pupil with the right parent!

Be sure to be up-to-date with details about children with special educational needs and/or learning difficulties. Some teachers will have a pile of pupils' work ready. This enables the teacher to illustrate remarks with a good piece of work, or to point out a weakness. Usually these meetings go well, but if any issues arise which cannot be resolved in the time available, you may need to suggest a follow-up meeting and to notify your head of department. Sometimes family problems will emerge and you may need to ask permission to pass details of these to other teachers.

What about relationships with parents outside school? Parents may genuinely be very grateful to you and ask you out to dinner, or to the opera, or to their holiday home for a weekend. This is fine, if the school is happy for you to do this – but you should check it first – as well as bearing in mind what was written about relationships with pupils in chapter 3; if it doesn't embarrass their child and provided there is no pressure on you to improve grades, give the child the leading role in *Hamlet*, make him captain of the 1st XI, or do something else that might be considered unprofessional.

I can remember, when teaching in the USA, being invited home for lunch – and after several glasses of very good wine, being asked to move their son's grade in English from a B to an A, as this would make his admission to Harvard much easier! Some parents may also give you a present at Christmas or at the end of the summer term. A bottle of wine or a box of chocolates is fine, but more valuable presents do sometimes appear, and at my last school it was policy for teachers to register any significant gifts with my office. My own favourite Christmas present from a tutee's parents was a large bunch of Irish mistletoe – it was very large and it filled the boot of their car!

Being invited to an 18th birthday party can be another pleasant gesture to you, and a vote of confidence in you, but again bear in mind the points made earlier in chapter 3 – especially if it is not at home or not at a venue supervised by parents, or if there is any danger of under-age drinking or drug abuse. You could easily be compromised. You also need to be careful not to drink too much alcohol, as this could lead to your making indiscreet remarks about the school or other colleagues.

Finally, there is always the chance encounter with parents outside school, at social events, in the street or even on holiday. I have bumped into parents and pupils unexpectedly in Sicily, Spain, Italy, Egypt, Zimbabwe, India and the USA. This goes with the job in an independent school. The pupil may be embarrassed or even horrified; the parents surprised but polite, but on occasions the parents may take the opportunity to lobby you about some issue at school. I once held up the check-out queue at Sainsbury's while a parent discussed her son's UCAS choices with me loudly and in detail. You just never know when...

Chapter 10

The role of the induction tutor

Lucy Leakey

Any NQT will be anticipating his or her induction period with both trepidation and excitement. Induction is perhaps one of the biggest learning curves of your teaching career. The responsibility, ownership and anonymity are on occasion quite overwhelming, but consistently incredibly rewarding. You may well be feeling anxious at the thought of starting your teaching post, but a big 'well done' for reaching this point – the start of your next journey.

As you embark on this new experience, don't ever underestimate how much you will be valued, the support you will be given and how much you will learn. It is an opportunity to meet new people, build relationships with staff, pupils and parents, and discover your own strengths. Perhaps the best part of this is that you will certainly not be facing any of it alone. Alongside you, throughout this period, will be your induction tutor (IT) and your colleagues. He/she/they will be sharing your experiences, guiding you through situations, offering advice and sharing your successes.

The height of my teaching career has without doubt been my time as IT. The privilege of being part of such an important and exciting time in an NQT's career is immeasurable. To see each one progress, build friendships and blossom, is probably as good as it gets.

To put this into some sort of context, I reflect on my own experience. When I started my first teaching post, in Cambridgeshire back in 1996, I still remember the feelings of anticipation, nerves and excitement. I was made to feel extremely welcome by all the established staff in my new school and I was well aware that, as I entered my first few days of being an NQT, I was surrounded by people who were supportive, friendly and informative.

Although I had a lot of advice offered from a wide variety of people, I certainly remember feeling at times as if I was not sure to whom I should be listening. I remember being observed on only one occasion throughout that first year, during a quiet reading period, and being told that everything was fine! I also recall consistently thinking 'Just how am I doing?' as there was seemingly nothing against which to measure my progress.

Fortunately I spent a very happy year at that school and, despite these anxieties, after 12 months I was deemed adequate enough to be given a full-term contract. Your induction (you will be pleased to know), will not be left to chance and fortune. The induction process in any walk of life should deal with the introduction of new staff to an existing working environment and the place of the employee within the organisation. It will have clear standards and targets, and be aiming towards a successful outcome.

In essence, an induction programme for NQTs is no different from any other. It should enable you, the NQT, to become fully integrated into the education establishment by whoever has employed you. It should treat you as a full and confident member of the team and it should provide evidence of the required statutory standards as set out by the DCSF and TDA and ISCtip. But above all, it should enable you to develop into a valued and competent teacher.

This chapter is based on a series of principles which will, I believe, facilitate the successful 'climate' of induction you would wish for as an NQT, and make it easier for you to make effective use of the induction process.

These principles are as follows:
- The role of the induction tutor should be well supported by the senior management team and recognised as important within the wider school context.
- Induction tutors should have had the opportunity to participate in relevant training offered by ISCtip, in turn developing the specific knowledge, skills and understanding required to carry out their responsibilities effectively.
- Everyone in the school who has contact with you as the NQT needs to recognise that they too are supporting the induction process, and

they too should also have a clear understanding of the role and responsibilities of the induction tutor.

I have had the opportunity to mentor several NQTs of different experiences and ages, from the raw recruit to the mature entrant with whom I am currently working. The experiences which I have encountered whilst doing so have given me a clear perspective on how a thriving induction programme needs to be carried out, to obtain maximum opportunity for success for all involved. Regardless of your background, age, experience and strengths, the key to a successful induction is, without doubt, a well structured, consistent and supportive partnership between the NQT and induction tutor.

As you will discover, the reality of being an NQT (or, indeed, an induction tutor) involves more than merely implementing the statutory induction arrangements. Your induction tutor should be working in different and distinct ways: supporting, evaluating, guiding, assessing, managing, coaching, and facilitating. (S)he will need to be able to tackle both anticipated and unexpected challenges, thus resolving any difficulties or conflicts which may arise, whilst providing you with thorough and sensitive feedback.

As an NQT, you may have more regular contact with those members of staff closely linked with you, such as a head of department or parallel teacher, and you will need to foster these relationships well and use the expertise they can offer, but it is your induction tutor who will provide the fundamental support throughout your NQT assessment period.

In summary, your induction tutor's key responsibilities will be:

- To inform the Head about your progress and contribute to the effective monitoring of your induction provision.
- To organise and facilitate appropriate and effective guidance and support for your professional development.
- To monitor carefully your progress towards a satisfactory completion of the induction, by gathering evidence and providing opportunities for fair and thorough assessments.
- To collaborate and liaise with all those involved in the induction process, both within and beyond the school.

The training provided by ISCtip for induction tutors is comprehensive and thorough. It provides clear guidelines in terms of standards, suggested timetables for induction and the requirements needed to be met by you, as the NQT, and your induction tutor.

It is important that you take the time to familiarise yourself with these standards and timetables, so that you know what to expect, but you should also take the first step in taking ownership of your own induction process. However, the materials and training courses provided by ISCtip are only part of the picture. As an NQT, your successful use of *all* the available sources of training and support will determine how much of a success your induction provision turns out to be.

From the perspective of the NQT, the induction tutor plays an enormously significant role during the first year of their teaching. Your induction tutor should be approachable, supportive and honest. It is important that a relationship of trust develops and that you begin to feel secure in the judgements and advice given to you. It is vital that you are provided with as much opportunity for success and development as is possible within the school, and that the induction process is as rich and varied as it can be.

I perceive the induction tutor's role to be vital in providing such a process, but do not forget that it is also up to you, as the NQT, to make constructive use of the guidance, standards and opportunities you are given, thus to a great extent determining your own success. In short, your responsibilities could be summarised as:

- Familiarising yourself with the process of induction, in particular the standards against which you will be measured.
- Participating proactively in your induction by making suggestions, showing initiative and acting upon advice given. Remind yourself that induction does not happen to you and that you are responsible for contributing to the process.
- Making use of your Career Entry and Development Profile (CEDP).
- Raising any concerns about the induction process, at any stage.

In order to fully benefit the school and yourself, some aspects of induction should have been planned in advance. A suitable member of staff will have agreed to take on the role of induction tutor and will ideally have met with you before the induction process starts. Many schools have a designated member of staff to coordinate induction arrangements across the school.

Those in such roles may not themselves be your personal induction tutor, for they may take responsibility for induction tutor preparation and quality assurance for *all* NQTs within a school. But whatever the specific arrangements in your school, all other staff should have been made aware of their own supporting roles and, more importantly for you, of precisely who is responsible for which aspects of induction.

In some cases, certain colleagues can provide a 'buddy system' for you. If possible this should be a person or persons with whom you will be working directly, and who can undertake some of the lighter tasks of the programme as well as generally making you feel welcome. Your induction tutor may have strengths and experience in other managerial roles or they may be recently qualified themselves. But, whatever the circumstances, the requirements of your induction tutor remain the same.

So, with what sort of experience can your induction tutor provide you? If a member of staff agrees to take on this role, at the very least (s)he should be well organised, communicative and capable of providing you, through his or her own performance, with a good role model. (S)he should be confident in helping you to develop your understanding of the characteristics of high quality teaching and learning, and in turn (s)he should recognise and develop your learning style. (S)he should also be assured in his or her own teaching ability and willing to allow you to observe the good practice arising from it.

Your induction tutor needs to have experience in making successful evaluations and observations. (S)he also needs to be open-minded and receptive to new ideas and approaches: remember that it is possible that you may have a more up-to-date knowledge of some teaching initiatives than your induction tutor! (S)he will need to be able to engage in positive dialogue with you and to work hard to foster a relationship of mutual trust and respect. But, above all, (s)he should be a good communicator and genuinely committed to supporting your development.

Where possible, induction tutors should have been given an allocation of non-contact time in order for them to carry out their role more effectively, and they should use this to spend regular, quality time with you. They should certainly have had the opportunity to participate in the appropriate training programme and they should without doubt enable you to feel comfortable in the structure and expectations of your induction programme.

In relation to planning and reviewing the induction programme they will also need to have full access to, and knowledge of, the school's policy documents which must be shared with you. They will require a thorough understanding of both the standards for the award of QTS, and the core standards, and a good knowledge of the resources available to support the induction programme and the requirements for satisfactory completion of the induction period.

Your initiative and professionalism is also vital to the success of your induction. I would expect an NQT to be as committed to fulfilling their potential as any induction tutor. You will be treated as a full-time member of the teaching team and your commitment to planning meetings, extra-curricular activities and work ethic should reflect this. It is a mutually creative and inter-sustaining process.

So, what type of opportunities can be provided for you as an NQT to enrich your induction programme and how can you ensure that you are given the opportunity to take a proactive part in your own induction? Before induction commences, I suggest you refer to the ISCtip *Evidence Checklist for Heads and Induction Tutors*. This document will enable you to see at a glance if all the necessary requirements (for you and for the school) are in place.

As an NQT you should be observed on a regular basis, both at an informal level to provide discussion and targets for the induction programme, and at a formal level to provide evidence of standards being achieved. I find it useful at the beginning of the first term of induction to draw together a timetable of observation and feedback opportunities with my NQTs. This is firmly centred around the yearly timetable for induction (support and monitoring), provided by ISCtip.

I usually do this a week or so into the first term, allowing a new teacher to get a feel for the role, before proceeding into lesson observations. I ask my NQTs to make suggestions as to when they would like to be watched: this is always a good starting point for the first couple of informal observations. It will also ensure that induction tutors make time for these formal observations to take place, and that an NQT has the opportunity to prepare fully for them.

The timetable should also include, where possible, opportunities for an NQT to make observations on other colleagues which will inform their own practice, and a slot for a vitally important weekly meeting, half-termly reviews and assessment meetings with your induction tutor. You may also wish to include on this timetable, the dates of any relevant NQT INSET provided by ISCtip or other courses that you and your induction tutor may feel are appropriate.

If your school or you have a contact in another school, suggest an opportunity to make a visit. Most schools are happy to facilitate such an experience and it will certainly enrich your own induction programme, besides enabling you to establish links beyond your own school community. Such a visit might be arranged to observe lessons and talk to an opposite number there. You may also wish to note on your timetable any relevant team planning meetings, parent evenings and school events of which you will be a part. Usually such a timetable evolves as the term progresses, but it is a great starting point for planning, and a copy should be kept as evidence in your NQT induction file.

When taking opportunities to observe other colleagues, a paired observation method can be used. This is particularly effective if you are looking to address a specific standard with your induction tutor. It involves arranging an opportunity for you both to complete a lesson observation on a colleague together.

Observing a lesson in this way provides a rich opportunity for discussion and a way to ensure that you get the most out of watching other colleagues using the various techniques of classroom management that are also known as the tricks of the trade! This paired method requires quality time together afterwards to discuss what you have seen and it is particularly helpful when looking in detail at a particular core standard.

As your confidence develops, you should be able to recognise the standards you are reaching, those you are working towards, and any which have not been addressed. You should be encouraged to collect evidence for your induction folder, to make detailed feedback on the formal self-evaluation forms and to collect notes and other documentation to support your progress.

The CEDP should be in evidence at your regular meetings and should be a reflection of the part you are playing in your own induction process. The formal assessment meetings, carried out each term, should be seen as an opportunity to summarise your progress to date. I have always used these meetings to look through all the standards, discuss any evidence and share the framework for the written report.

The objectives, action plans and long term aims, which should also be summarised at such a meeting, form the next part of the induction process. Success criteria need to be laid out clearly, so that improvements can be identified and acknowledged. Early recognition of difficulties is always in the interest of both you and your induction tutor; so while it is vital that your successes be acknowledged, you should not be unnerved if an area for development, or even the occasional weakness, is discussed in a sensitive and constructive manner. Indeed, induction tutors take a lot of care with the wording of observation summaries and review meeting records. Keeping minutes of each meeting that you have together ensures that there is written evidence of both successes and difficulties and how these have been celebrated or addressed.

Finally, it is important to remember that it is the process, not the paperwork, which is at the heart of a good induction. The opportunities to discuss a morning's work over lunch or a cup of tea are perhaps the most valuable; as an NQT, make sure that you invest your time wisely. Endless lesson plans and observations are not going to enrich your development, but a variety of different experiences will.

Get involved in school life in its broadest sense: ask for opportunities for peer observations; work towards setting up school visits; participate in the extracurricular life of the school, and go to the pub with the other staff on a Friday! I have no doubt that whether you are experienced in industry or fresh out of training college, you will find induction occasionally frustrating and time-consuming but, in essence, hugely rewarding. Be honest, well organised, use the support available – and, above all, always smile.

Chapter 11

Those who work around you

John Baugh

It's Day One of your teaching career. You have been issued with your laptop, had umpteen pre-term meetings, tried to make your classroom as welcoming as possible, headed up your mark-book and prepared your lessons as far ahead, it seems, as Christmas. The phoney war is over. Let battle commence. You decide to get in to work as early as possible without it looking as if you have camped there overnight. You take a flask of coffee and some chocolate brownies – just to ease your nerves. Let's look at two possible scenarios.

Scenario one: as you park your car (assuming that you have one) in the near-empty staff car park and make your way to your classroom, you notice signs of life. You pass someone jangling a large bunch of keys and you nod politely. A cleaner is just finishing off the vacuuming in your classroom. You smile and busy yourself by unpacking your laptop, coffee and brownies – she leaves. A short while later, you hear sounds of life in the next door classroom and you get up to close the door. Later still, children begin to arrive – at last, someone to talk to.

Scenario two: as you park your car in the near-empty staff car park and make your way to your classroom, you notice signs of life. You pass someone jangling a large bunch of keys and you say "good morning" whilst introducing yourself. This starts a short conversation on the weather and the fortunes of Newcastle United Football Club.

A cleaner is just finishing off the vacuuming in your classroom. You smile, say good morning, ask if she minds your getting in her way and say thank you when she leaves. A short while later, you hear sounds of life in the next door classroom and you get up to investigate. You find a colleague struggling to carry several boxes of books and papers and you offer to help. Moments later you are sharing a cup of coffee and a chocolate brownie. Later still, children begin to arrive.

It isn't difficult to see what has happened here and where the future lies for you if either of these scenarios sets a pattern for the rest of the day, the week, the term or your career. The title of this chapter is: 'Those who work around you.' It isn't 'Those who work for you' or 'Those who work below you'. You won't go far wrong if you begin by respecting the work of each and every member of the school community, and by going out of your way to learn their names and a little of their lives. The simple fact that the caretaker knows that you are someone who will stop and chat about the lack of a decent goalkeeper will – believe me – make all the difference one day. The fact that he knows that you are not another one of those 'stuck-up teachers' really matters.

Your new school is full of people who will, at some point or another, have a significant impact on your life. It's a complex ecosystem and no matter how large or small your school, there is likely to be a natural order to it. Now is the time to try and untangle the web.

The Big Beasts

Somewhere out there are likely to be the governors. These are hand-picked pillars of society who act as non-executive trustees of the school. They are likely to take their role very seriously and a few of them will be more visible than others. Some may be current parents and it is these that you will probably get to know best. If you are really (un)lucky, you may find that you teach one of their children. Find out whether this is the case – it's best to be forewarned.

Governors are often very busy and successful people in their own lines of business and do not have a lot of time to devote to visiting the school or getting to know each and every intimate detail. They have to support the Head, the bursar and the management team without interfering in the running of the school. They are legally responsible for everything that goes on and yet they are not able – or at least they shouldn't be able – to pull very many strings.

Good governors trust the school management to run the school and in many ways it's best that they keep looking at the bigger picture. Although they may appear distant and remote, try not to join in with the inevitable chorus of: "Who are the governors anyway? You never see them around." They are likely to know more about the school than most people realise and, to be fair, any time they give to the school should be appreciated and valued. One further piece of advice: try not to buttonhole governors about grievances or complaints. The school should have a proper procedure for this and it isn't good form to bypass the proper lines of communication.

More Big Beasts

Closer to hand, but perhaps just as elusive, will be the Head and the senior management team. You will want to speak to these people at some point and you shouldn't worry about making yourself known. Almost every Head I have met has welcomed new staff popping into their office or enjoyed bumping into them around the school. It gives them a chance to find out how you are getting on without having to seek you out. Don't make a nuisance of yourself, but let the Head know you are enjoying working at the school (assuming you are) and thank him or her for appointing you.

If you have worries or concerns, make sure you take them to the right person. This could be a deputy head (academic or pastoral), your head of department, the member of staff responsible for NQT mentoring or the bursar. Cross your fingers and hope that some of these have an open door policy; otherwise be prepared to make appointments. Remember that these are busy people and they are hard at it with things that few other people see or understand. The Head is the chief executive and the bursar is his or her right hand (wo)man; everything rests on their shoulders so try not to add to their stress levels if you can.

In larger schools, you are more likely to deal on a day-to-day basis with the deputy head than the Head. A good deputy head will act as a conduit between staff and the Head and you should assume that the deputy head will be reporting back on a regular basis. It would be wise to ask the deputy head to keep certain things confidential if you really do not want the Head to know, and this they should do unless they feel that you, another member of staff or a pupil, is at risk of harm.

Some schools may have more than one deputy head and it is important to try and determine the specific role that each plays. One deputy may be responsible for academic matters (also known as the director of studies) and he or she will be the person to see if you have concerns about your teaching load or balance. (You might also consider speaking to your head of department first.) There may also be a deputy in charge of pastoral matters and he or she would help answer queries on matters such as bullying and relationships. (Again, you may like to take these matters to the head of year concerned in the first instance.)

A word on the bursar and a chance to mix our metaphors: the school can be seen as a large ship and the Head is the captain. However, this ship needs to be kept afloat, maintained, resourced and the crew fed and paid. This is what the bursar does – not personally, of course, but it's all his or her big toy to play with. The bursar's job description will be one of the longest in the school and will – with some variations – fall under the following headings:

- **Finance** (budgeting; monitoring income and expenditure; collecting all fees and other dues; debt management; the payment of all salaries and wages; scrutinising and passing for payment all invoices and statements of account; preparing financial appraisals of particular projects; advising on taxation; advising on the financial implications of the charitable status of the school; administering pension schemes for teaching and other staff; managing bursary and scholarship funds.)
- **Administration** (maintaining employees' personal files and records; employment legislation; health and safety; risk assessments; maintaining contact with the statutory authorities and with other organisations; supervising the school's insurance in all its forms and ensuring adequate cover for all relevant risks; acting as clerk and secretary to the governors.)
- **School buildings and grounds** (maintenance and security of the school buildings; installation and maintenance of equipment for protection against and escape from fire; maintenance and efficiency of the installations and plant for electric supply; heating; domestic hot water; cooking; water-softening, *etc*; supervision of the lighting and ventilation of the school buildings; production of outline specifications for new buildings; obtaining tenders; planning

permission; liaison with architects; upkeep of playing fields, gardens, all-weather surfaces, running tracks and tennis courts, *etc.*)
• **Staff** (selection, appointment, deployment and management of the non-teaching staff of the school.)

As you can see, this is a busy and important person – and this list is far from complete.

There is a danger sometimes that the bursar and the Head are known to disagree on certain matters. Whatever you do, don't try and take advantage of this and wangle something from the bursar that the Head has already said no to – or *vice versa*. Nothing is likely to upset one or the other more than having their authority challenged in this way. It's also perfectly likely that the Head and the bursar are close and loyal colleagues and that their united front creates confidence to all around them.

Somewhere in this array of characters could well be the Head's spouse. These days, he or she is increasingly likely to have a full- or part-time job outside the school, especially in a day school. However, depending on the size and nature of the school, this person could well develop into being an important person in your life. This is more likely to be the case for boarding and prep schools and – since the majority of their world still seems to work this way – if the spouse is a woman. So let us assume that we are talking about the Head's wife and one who may be fully employed by the school to fulfil a range of jobs. From here you can then scale down the importance of the role according to what you find in your new school.

The Head's wife may well be responsible for many of the domestic arrangements in the school, such as supervising the catering and managing matrons and health staff. She may also take some part in meeting prospective parents and being part of the public face of the school. She is likely to know all the governors well and will probably have a handle on most, if not all, of the parents. Most significantly she has the ear of your boss and you would be well advised to create a good impression from Day One.

Smaller but Important Beasts
An institution stands or falls on the quality of its middle management and

the effectiveness of communication through its members – either up or down. It is these people, the heads of year, the heads of departments and the houseparents who really know what is going on in the school: you should listen to them carefully. A good school has really good people in these positions and they should be setting the tone – led from above – as to how things need to be done.

If you have academic concerns or questions about the curriculum, ask your head of department; if your worries are more of a pastoral nature and concern a pupil's progress or state of mind, ask the head of year. Keep them informed, ideally by short emails, of things that you think they should know and it's a kindness to them to suggest that they needn't reply if it's not necessary.

Each school has its own management structure and this can be complex – even confusing – in large schools. Try to get a handle on how things work early on and if in doubt – ask.

Lesser Beasts to ignore at your peril

Every thriving ecosystem has a diverse and abundant range of beings further down the ladder. The organisation depends on each of these to carry out specific and important functions and without them the system falters. Many of these people are easily identified as teachers or teaching assistants and their positions need no explanation. That said, these are likely to be your closest colleagues, friends and confidants – so bide your time and remain friendly with a degree of polite reserve.

As for all the others, they all have their place. Take a little time to get to know their names if you can and show a respect for the work they do. It is not necessary to explain the obvious duties of those who clean the school, cook the meals or wash the dishes but I suggest you set yourself a little challenge. See how many of these people you can name by the end of your first term. Of course, the bigger the school, the bigger the challenge but I would be concerned if you weren't able to meet and greet some of these people by name after a few weeks.

Before we finish, there is one very important member of staff that needs to be identified and this is the child protection officer – sometimes called the safeguarding officer. One of your greatest responsibilities as a teacher is the protection of children, and you have an obligation to learn and understand the child protection procedures of your new school. You should receive training in this as part of your induction and if this is not forthcoming, you should ask.

The school's child protection officer may be the Head but this is becoming less common these days so it is more likely to be a deputy head or senior member of staff. It is their job to handle all child protection matters and if you don't know who they are and what they do, you cannot help in the protection of children.

Starting a new career is an exciting and challenging proposition. To mis-quote former President Clinton, always remember "It's the people, stupid." Teaching is not a career in which you can plough a lone furrow. Your new colleagues – whether Big Beasts or Tiny Minnows – all have an impact on you and you on them. Also, don't forget the most important people of all – the group that this chapter hardly mentions at all. The pupils. Learn to respect them and they will respect you. Like so much of what is contained here, it's really that simple.

Perhaps the best way to end is by considering scenario three: it's late in the evening and you return to school after a long day away with a sports team. You need to pick up some books from your classroom as the evening will have to involve some crucial marking for tomorrow. The classrooms are locked and there are no signs of life. You know the number of the caretaker who lives nearby. Do you phone?

I expect the answer to that depends on whether you lived through scenario one or scenario two.

Chapter 12

Input and output: admissions and public exams

Michael Punt

This chapter aims to give you a bird's eye view of several areas of school life in which you are unlikely to be directly involved in the very first stage of your career, but which have an important effect on the conditions in which you work. Pupils are a school's *raison d'être* – something that we should never forget. So how are they brought in, and what do they hope to achieve in academic terms as they emerge on their way out?

You arrive at your classroom on day one to be greeted by your first group of pupils. How have they come to be there? How were they chosen? You will have a range of data available to you about your pupils, and it is important that you take full advantage of this. It may include entrance test results and rank orders of candidates, reports from previous schools, aptitude or value added tests taken within your school and previous end-of-term reports. Your induction tutor should be able to explain how any value-added testing takes place in your school, and the uses to which the school puts it.

Some schools are, of course more selective than others in academic terms. The most fiercely academic will have more than their share of apparent geniuses, but even within these schools there will be a spread of ability. Other schools (and the classes within them) will contain pupils from across quite a wide ability range. Never assume that the child at the bottom of the class is struggling purely because he or she doesn't work – at least, not until you have checked your information systems.

Marketing

Independent schools have to market themselves in a competitive climate.

Prospective parents have to be convinced that the product they are being offered is so irresistible that they will be prepared to forego the maintained sector place for which they have already paid through their taxes, preferring instead to pay fees to your school – and sometimes making big sacrifices, including new cars and holidays, in the process – and that they will choose your school rather than the rival independent school down the road.

A declining number of children go to a school because their parents went there; an increasing number don't automatically send their younger child to the school which their elder one attended. A growing number chop and change between sectors: for example, many schools can no longer take for granted that Year 11 pupils will go on through into Year 12. These trends vary in degree from area to area of course, but taken together they all point to the need for very effective marketing.

In many schools the admissions season lasts for nearly the entire academic year, beginning with Open Days, but including interview days, visits on 'normal' working days, scholarship assessments and entrance exams. For all parties – pupils, parents and schools – it can be a stressful time, but it is important that pupils who join any school ultimately find themselves in an institution where they are happy and able to flourish.

In many areas of the country, pupils apply to join several maintained and independent schools (five or six is not uncommon). They and their parents may decide to accept an offer because of a whole variety of factors: reputation; cost; location; friends' choice; and the instinctive feel of the school (does the pupil-school fit seem right?). The quality and friendliness of the admissions process itself plays a part in this. Good prospectuses, websites and promotional DVDs all count. In most cases, parents will also meet with the relevant Head or deputy so that they have the opportunity to ask questions.

As a very general rule, applications to schools at ages up to 11 are mostly parent-led. At 13+, prep schools (and their Heads) tend to have a big role in advising parents on the best school for their child (especially in the boarding sector). At 16+, especially in areas with strong sixth-form colleges, schools tend to market themselves as much to the would-be pupil or student as to the parent and (as you may recall from your own experience) it is a rare parent who can go completely against the wishes of his/her offspring.

Where candidates are making multiple applications, schools offer more places than there are spaces, and this ratio of offers to likely acceptances can be a difficult judgement to make. Many a Head will gain a few extra wrinkles or grey hairs during the admissions season, but never ask them to admit it!

While some pupils may transfer between schools during the course of their school education, others could remain in the same institution from the age of three to 18. Those meeting the nervous little boy or girl who is more interested in the welcome biscuit than whether (s)he gains admission to the sought-after pre-prep school, might wonder whether that individual will one day be leaving the sixth form with a glittering array of prizes *en route* to a highly prestigious university. Pupils change.

In this situation, while most pupils and parents would like to hope that transfer through one school with several sections (pre-prep, prep and senior) would be automatic, schools will often expect pupils to reach certain standards at certain stages. Some schools expect pupils to sit entrance exams alongside external candidates to move, say, from Year 6 to Year 7. Some might make this a deliberate hurdle; others use this only as a benchmarking exercise to compare external candidates and existing pupils with their places guaranteed.

Usually, if there is likely to be an issue over transfer between the stages, parents would be warned at least a year ahead, and teachers who know their pupils well enough should be able to identify those for whom a move elsewhere might be in their best interests. This tends to be the exception rather than the rule though, and is most likely to be the order of the day only in the most academically-focused schools.

Entrance procedures

Independent schools will select in different ways but parents may ask for a copy of the school's admissions policy so that they can understand the basis on which their child may or may not be offered a place. There are no hard and fast rules as to what the process might be at each of the key admission stages, but here are some examples of how the majority of schools select their intake.

1. Reception
   - Play-based activities to see how children might interact with each other.
   - One-to-one assessment of each child which may include some basic literacy and numeracy tasks.

2. Year 3

By this stage pupils have attended school for at least three years; thus more can be expected of them and a school reference gives information as to how they have performed so far. Selection may therefore be based on:

   - An interview – perhaps including an assessment of reading or arithmetic.
   - School reference.
   - Performance in entrance tests – maths, English and reasoning (verbal or non-verbal).
   - A classroom activity to see how seven year-olds interact with each other.

3. Year 7

Entry at this stage probably follows a similar format to that at Year 3. Given that this is when many primary school children would naturally transfer to a senior secondary, the numbers involved can be very large. However the selection may be based on:

   - An interview.
   - School reference.
   - Entrance test performance – maths, English and reasoning (verbal or non-verbal).
   - Some schools use the Common Entrance exam (see the next section).

4. Year 9

Entry may be similar to those above, with papers set by the school applied to, possibly including a science or modern languages paper as well.

Some schools, especially those with boarders, may use the Common Entrance examinations for entry at 13+ or 11+, which are set by the Independent Schools Examinations Board, but the papers are marked by the senior school to which the candidate has applied. Most candidates sit the papers in their existing school (UK or overseas) and all take papers in English, maths and science. They may also offer papers in French, geography, German, Greek, history, Latin, religious studies, and Spanish at 13+. In addition, a school reference would be supplied and the candidate is likely to be interviewed. There is no overall moderation of results, the senior school making its own decisions as to which pupils it takes.

5. The sixth form

An offer of a sixth-form place is often based on:

- School reference.
- Interview.
- Satisfactory performance at GCSE. A school with strong competition for places might, for example, ask for a minimum of six grade As with at least As in subjects to be taken at sixth form level, but for many others something nearer to six Bs might be the order of the day.

At some of these entry stages, schools may offer scholarships to the candidates who demonstrate the greatest academic ability and potential. These may simply go to those who perform best in the selection criteria above, or there may be an extra set of interviews, group activities, or papers to be sat, depending on the school. Many schools have scaled down the value of scholarships in recent years, preferring to offer means-tested bursaries to talented pupils who would not otherwise be able to afford to join them.

Even though the various components of the selection process allow candidates to demonstrate different strengths, a school might still try to take other factors into account if possible. Has a child been tutored for years simply to gain entry at 11+, meaning that their performance may well have peaked?

Does the reference suggest that (s)he might thrive more in a bigger/smaller school, regardless of academic ability? Has the child come from a difficult home situation or disadvantaged school, meaning that although the interview performance was unpolished and the test scores mediocre, there was that *special something* indicating that (s)he had considerable undeveloped potential?

Like the best universities, many schools have more good candidates than there are places, but all work hard to ensure that the admissions process is fair, careful and friendly. In recent years this aim has become more complex, owing to the growing proliferation of public exams which independent school pupils take.

Universities tend to divide into those which are in the position of being able to select undergraduates and those which have to recruit them. Those in the former category also find themselves under pressure to make every allowance for the extent to which a candidate's achievements have been affected (for good or ill) by the quality or otherwise of his/her school: a frequently contentious issue, aired extensively in the press.

Public examinations

Independent schools are fortunate in that they are free to set their own curriculum, and the public examinations taken at key stages within that curriculum may or may not be the same as those within the maintained sector. The choice of examinations is growing and there is something of a 'pick and mix' culture developing which might, from the outside, appear untidy but which at the same time allows Heads and curriculum leaders the flexibility to choose courses that are appropriate to the needs of the students within a school, or within a department. Probably, the larger the institution, the greater may be the range of courses offered and therefore the greater the mix of public examinations taken.

It is also said that simply weighing a pig does not make it fatter, and young people in UK schools can be some of the most tested pupils in the world – some might say over-tested. Perhaps the guiding principles which govern the examination course(s) chosen in any given school are:

- Does it fit the needs of the pupils? Does it interest and challenge and does it allow teachers the flexibility to teach in a way that allows them to deliver their subject in a way that is appealing to their pupils? Is there mind-numbing coursework that involves more hoop-jumping than independent thinking?

- Will the course be a recognised passport to the next stage? Does the GCSE prepare for A level? Do the sixth-form courses offered have a well-regarded currency with the universities that the sixth formers aspire to attend?

- Can the examination courses be taken in any combination of subjects (timetable permitting) or are there specified combinations of subjects to enforce breadth?

- Do the examinations accurately measure the progress made by the pupils over the duration of the course? Teachers in our schools often follow interesting tangents; they do not stick rigidly to narrow specifications and they are encouraged, as are their pupils, to be original thinkers. When it comes to the examinations, is this a help or hindrance, and do the examinations provide a useful end point to the course?

The choice of public examinations that our pupils sit may therefore include (at the time of writing):

1. Primary
   a) KSI SATS – national curriculum tests taken at the end of Year 2 in core subjects/skills specified by the government.

   b) KS2 SATS – national curriculum tests taken at the end of Year 6 in core subjects/skills.

2. Pre-16
   a) GCSEs – offered by a handful of examination boards: Edexcel, AQA and OCR; WJEC in Wales and CCEA in Northern Ireland (which is part of the Education Skills Authority there); usually taken at the end

of Year 11 but sometimes earlier in some subjects. Increasingly the examinations are becoming modular so that papers may be sat as early as Year 9 and there remains a coursework element. Typically, pupils take up to ten GCSEs.

b) IGCSEs – (International GCSEs) are growing in popularity, particularly in maths, science and English. They are only offered by Edexcel and CIE exam boards, and are taken throughout the schools. Sometimes regarded as more traditional (or rigorous), some schools find they are a better preparation for A level and more challenging for brighter pupils. They are not currently included in government performance tables.

c) IB Middle Years Programme – (International Baccalaureate) is being offered by a small but growing number of schools in a curriculum that operates up to Year 11. There are eight subject groups linked to a core, and teachers organise continuous assessment tasks over the programme to give grades which may be validated by the International Baccalaureate (IB).

3. Post-16

a) A level – which is invariably modular and comprises two or three modules taken in Year 12 (AS) and two or three further modules taken in Year 13 (A2). AS is less difficult than A2 but each year counts towards half of the total score. A level offers a free choice of subject.

b) The Pre-U – is a relatively new qualification offered by CIE designed specifically as a preparation for university studies. There is a free choice of subject, with three principal subjects taken and exams taken at the end of the two-year course. There is also the opportunity for students to produce an independent report. Currently schools offering the Pre-U may offer it alongside other courses.

c) IB Diploma Programme – has also been growing in popularity and many schools offer it either alongside or instead of A level. Students study six subjects taken from subject groups (three at higher level and three at standard level); there is an extended essay, a theory of knowledge component, and participation in CAS (creativity, action and service) is expected as part of the diploma. IB exams are taken at the end of the two-year course.

d) The AQA Baccalaureate (AQABacc) aims to test a similar range of skills, including subject study in depth, critical thinking and independent learning, personal development, citizenship and community service.

e) In Scotland pupils take Standard Grade and Intermediate exams at or around age 15 to 16, followed by Highers and Advanced Highers at sixth-form level.

f) At the time of writing (2009) no independent schools in England offer the government's Diploma courses, but a handful are considering introducing these qualifications at Advanced Level.

It would appear that the number of curriculum options, and therefore public examinations, may continue to grow. While this offers a greater degree of choice for pupils and their parents choosing schools, it means that the system, from the outside, appears even more complicated. Even within the existing structure, our schools are including their own awards or diplomas alongside the externally recognised qualifications.

If you have taken public exams in a day school in the UK in recent years, you will of course be familiar with the razzmatazz surrounding 'results day'. You will probably remember your own experience of that day very clearly: how your school handled the news it gave you, and those of your contemporaries who were either ecstatic or despairing about their grades. For independent day schools (and maintained sector schools too), it is a day unlike any other in the school year.

On that day many independent schools are often also involved in giving out news about results to the local press, and in compiling data which will be collated centrally and given to the national press, which then tends to turn them into league tables. These have been in existence for two decades now, yet they remain very controversial.

League tables

These vary in form from one newspaper to another each August – again complicated by the existence of several different public exams, and the relative weight which the different tariffs (in particular, the UCAS tariff) give to each one. Schools dislike them, but they cannot ignore them: parents take notice of them (even though many are more sophisticated in their reading of the data than was once the case).

Some schools try to frustrate the efforts of the compilers by declining to publish their results, but the majority seem to take the view that, however flawed the tables may be, it is counterproductive to be seen to be trying to hide their results in an age when the public sets high store by freedom of information. However, the prolonged refusal by the government to include IGCSE results in the school performance tables (which it produces each year after the exam results season is over) has effectively thwarted the public, because an increasing number of independent schools – including some of those who achieve the highest exam results in the UK – regard it almost as a badge of honour to score their 'nil' in the five A*-E GCSE performance tables.

Why are these tables flawed in other ways? Predominantly because until someone is able to devise a system which calculates value added achievement in a way which nobody disputes, a school's results will always be dictated to a large extent by the ability of the pupils which it admits – and especially by the level of its 'bottom' 25%.

Furthermore, some schools in both sectors 'play the system', discouraging pupils at a late stage from sitting for exams which they may struggle with, or resorting to exams which have spuriously high tariff weightings. It is also because (especially in a small sixth form) the results of the candidate who has appalling hay fever on the day or who has been struggling through the year with emotional, family or other difficulties can have a significant bearing on a school's overall percentage figures at (say) grades A and B.

As you contemplate your classes early in the autumn term, the detail of many of these issues lies ahead for you – but probably not for a while yet. You should aim to keep up with new developments in all these qualifications though, either through your department and your school, or via the various exam board websites. Meanwhile, it should be our prime concern to keep all pupils busy, challenged and interested.

Chapter 13

Balances and checks

Chris Brown

Appraisal, performance management and inspection

As an NQT, you, dear reader, are much more fortunate than your supposed elders and betters. Your training has ensured that you have been given more practical instruction in such issues as classroom management and lesson planning than those of us trained some years ago. Your teaching practice will have been more diverse.

Furthermore, you have been repeatedly exposed to your lessons being observed. Certainly when I started out on my first teaching job, induction was minimal – as was any observation of what I did, except from a discreet distance and perhaps by that form of osmosis that is practised in schools. Now, as a retired Head who does a good deal of appraisal of Heads and senior staff, I still come across senior teachers who have not become used to another adult being present in the lesson and have only been appraised for the first time in their later years.

Most schools within the principal independent school associations use ISCtip as the means by which new staff are accredited as teachers. This process necessarily brings with it mentoring, advice from within a department and from a senior teacher, and also regular observation of your lessons, together with constructive suggestions for improvement. It is a much more open and supportive process than hitherto.

In addition, many schools have worked actively to create a climate where mutual observation is the norm, and where you can observe others, share ideas and materials, as well as being observed yourself. Furthermore, most schools offer induction into the nature and idiosyncrasies of their particular establishment.

Independent schools still have the freedom to employ those who do not have a teaching qualification, perhaps because they switched to teaching later in life or decided on a career change. In any event, nowadays you can gain QTS whilst on the job by means of a graduate training scheme (GTP), or by distance learning. Those within the school again perform an important role in mentoring and guiding. Your route into the profession may not be conventional. There is nothing wrong with that; schools need such diversity.

It is not always easy to draw a clear line between appraisal and performance management. Often there can be a blurring at the edges. The essential difference, however, is that appraisal explores the needs and aspirations of the individual; performance management looks to direct the teacher to develop, improve or change as the school wishes. As an NQT you may not also be required to be appraised in your first year. The practice varies.

Appraisal systems

Once within your first job, you will probably find an appraisal process in place. Appraisal has been a part of most schools for some years now, but it is fair to say that most schemes have been revised repeatedly. It is also the case that appraisal of senior managers and Heads is now undertaken. The latter are themselves within schools where all other teachers are subject to the process and think it proper that they should be too. It is usually felt inappropriate for someone within an organisation to do the task, so often an outsider undertakes it. HMC, for example, has a list of several retired Heads who do such work.

A good appraisal scheme is one which ensures that the quality of teaching and learning is central to the process, with observation of a lesson or lessons. Some self-evaluation is also important, so that you can reflect on what has gone well, and what less well. You might expect to be asked what your aims are for the coming term or year. Since independent schools pride themselves on the quality of their pastoral care and the range of opportunity outside the classroom, a good appraisal scheme also allows for your contribution in these areas to be understood and valued, as well as evaluated.

Most schemes may offer targets for the coming year, which of course should be clear and attainable. The opportunity for further training should also be part of the discussion. Schools run their own INSET but relevant courses are offered by IAPS (for prep schools), ISA and HMC/GSA/SHMIS (for senior schools) under the aegis of their training arm, the organisation of Independent Professional Development (IPD). Many other providers also exist. For your benefit and development, it is important that you take advantage of what is helpful and relevant to develop your skills and qualifications, be it in assessment for learning, IT, or mountain leadership.

Most appraisal systems look to ensure that teachers are appraised annually but some may offer different degrees of thoroughness or lightness of touch over, say, a three-year cycle. Many will start with the head of department but will then be managed by a more senior teacher or a member of SMT, before leading to an interview with the Head. In some schools, the Head will be involved annually; in others, not.

One important issue about appraisal is its manageability. If the process is admirably thorough and detailed, drawing views from a range of colleagues and with several lesson observations, then it may become too burdensome, and some systems founder because in a busy life finding the necessary time can be difficult.

The Holy Grail is a system that both serves its purpose but is manageable rather than oppressive. It is not an easy balance to strike. Good practice will always see lesson observation as its cornerstone, and the school and departmental development plans as the umbrella under which it sits.

An essential tension exists in appraisal. Who is it for? Systems seek to support individuals, their concerns and aspirations, but also to act as a means of performance management by the Head or senior managers, or indeed governors. If a Head is seeking to address parental concerns, aim for a better academic results or a fuller contribution to extracurricular activities, then that purpose, however understandable, can place less focus on the wishes and concerns of the individual.

Many systems manage that tension well; some less so. I know of one school which specifically separates the two, so any performance management issue, from irregular marking to unpunctuality to, in the extreme, lack of competence, is dealt with by the relevant head of department, member of SMT or indeed the Head, whilst the appraisal system is much more 'person-centred'.

This separation avoids the conflict that can otherwise exist. I have to confess that as a Head, I was at times more concerned about the former function than the latter, which was not always as it should be. At least one school uses professionals from outside for appraisal, which enables a greater clarity in dividing the two aspects.

When all is said and done, appraisal is key to ensuring that a teacher is given time and space to reflect on how things are going; given the attention and experience of others; and encouraged to think about aims for the future, both short term and career based; and as a result to consider appropriate training. It can be an exciting as well as demanding process, if well managed. It is also a moment when affirmation and praise can be given; these are not necessarily the diet of every day. What better way to contemplate the coming term than with encouragement and praise ringing in your ears.

Performance management

Performance management has also been approached through salary structures. In the broadest sense, individuals within a school have traditionally been rewarded by promotion. The good rise young. As the state system looked to enhance the salary of teachers, the notion of thresholds arose: bars on the salary scale that could only be crossed if certain standards of teaching and contribution were achieved. In the early stages, it became apparent that most within the state sector were admitted to the higher level, which in turn led to a second round of thresholds.

The independent sector responded to this variously. Some schools wished to avoid excessive bureaucracy and 'box-ticking'. Some schools saw it as an opportunity to introduce demands for such entitlement, perhaps particularly in relation to extracurricular contribution or boarding duties. Others felt that contributions to the life of independent schools were diverse and not entirely comparable. How, for instance, can you compare coaching a team with producing a play, or taking an exchange group to Spain with looking after lost property? All contribute; collegiality is a concept to be valued rather than giving small incremental points for every activity or responsibility.

The management of performance by salary and incentive is thus very differently treated by differing schools. A very broad generalisation suggests that in the past longer-established boarding schools often had very long incremental scales with relatively few other posts of responsibility; day schools often had shorter scales more closely aligned to those of the state sector. Nowadays some give an allowance to acknowledge that all contribute beyond the minimum; others favour a sophisticated points system; some have both. Some have bars on the salary scale that are demanding to cross; others a straight forward progression.

Long salary scales with small but inexorable steps have mostly gone. Many more reflect the structure within the state sector, not least since many teachers look to see what is happening elsewhere. As a young teacher, it is only prudent for you to understand the structure in your school and whether you are fairly treated. One advantage, arguably of several, that Heads in independent schools have is that when appointing an individual, judgement can be used in where that person joins the scale, to acknowledge particular experience or years beyond qualification for teaching or your university degree. A state school Head generally has less freedom for manoeuvre. The expectation of your role should also be clearly laid out in your job description.

Increasingly, heads of department have been expected to be middle managers, and not simply *primus inter pares*. Inspection particularly has often pointed to the variable standards of management across departments in a given school. I suspect that this may still be the case, and something which you may experience. The expectation is that in a large secondary school, a head of department will be responsible for those within his or her department, as their line manager.

That role means not just selecting texts or chairing meetings, but ensuring standards of teaching and marking are good, or that punctuality is as it should be, that indeed competence in the role is of a professional standard; that the progression of the career for a new teacher is considered and opportunities offered. Your immediate superior may be excellent; he or she may also be delightful and less than exemplary. If the latter is the case, it is difficult for you to do other than seek a member of the SMT or other senior teacher who can help and advise you. It is an issue you may be able to raise in appraisal.

Inspection

The recent history of inspections in independent schools raises some interesting questions about what inspection should look for, and how it should be carried out. It may be helpful for a moment to see how matters have developed.

Inspection of schools took a significant change with the creation of the Office for Standards in Education, Children's Services and Skills (Ofsted), and thus the systematic and public evaluation of a school's performance. Up until that time such matters were more discreetly overseen by Her Majesty's Inspectors (HMI). Independent schools have always been required to meet certain standards if they are to be recognised and registered by the government department responsible for education (known at the time of writing as the Department for Children, Schools and Families [DCSF]).

This public change and accountability led the independent sector to think how it might best respond, and a little history serves to focus our minds on the issue of what an inspection is, or should be, all about.

IAPS and GSA had offered a quality audit of schools but it was not focused on the classroom; HMC felt a different step was needed and created its own system modelled on Ofsted; the latter approved. This ran for a six year cycle from 1993-9, but by the later '90s it seemed only sensible for a structure to be created for all schools in the associations gathered within the Independent Schools Council. The first Blair administration enacted this in law, so the Independent Schools Inspectorate (ISI) was created in 1999.

Its process was similar to that of Ofsted, and indeed it is monitored by that body. Its Lead Inspectors (now called Reporting Inspectors) were usually former HMI or recently retired Heads of independent schools. A critical difference from Ofsted was that the team inspectors were principally teachers from other such schools who, once trained, offered to inspect once a year.

A modest payment was offered, but not a fee; more an acknowledgement than a payment commensurate to the demands of the role. These inspectors were after all being paid by their schools and the spirit of reciprocity was important. They also had (and still have) the advantage that they themselves are fresh from the classroom and understand the difficulties encountered. It was, and is, an outstanding form of in-service training. You are privileged to look within every aspect of a school, to see that matters can be successfully run in differing ways, and you are also asked to be objective in your evaluation of what you see.

The first cycle of such inspections ran from 1999 until 2005, and all schools in ISC were inspected under this regime. The framework employed required that whole school issues be examined (such as teaching, pupil welfare, or governance and management), but also that reports on individual subjects were given. Every teacher, full or part-time would be observed at least once.

Meanwhile thinking in the wider world of education had moved on. Ofsted's examination of state schools led to the accumulation of a lot of data about them, and so it was felt less necessary to inspect in such depth in all cases. If a school functioned well, it was seen as not so necessary; those which were a cause for concern, however, might be placed in 'Special Measures' and visited more often. Recognising this development, schools served by ISI thus felt that a 'lighter touch system' should be devised for independent schools, too.

Within that second cycle system (2005-9), no inspection of subjects was undertaken. The focus was much more on 'whole school issues', so the report would speak of teaching but not, for example, of English or history teaching. Many teachers found (still find) it strange that inspection could be taking place around them but that they were not themselves observed. The team undertaking the inspection was smaller and spent a day less in the school than previously. Monday to Thursday was the norm, rather than the Monday to Friday arrangements of the first cycle.

The resultant report looked to summarise prominently what the school does well and what next steps it must take to improve in response to certain judgements. Schools must respond to the latter and indicate how such issues will be addressed. It is also important to underline that the process looks at all the regulations by which schools must abide, from health and safety to child protection, from the standard of buildings to registration. Failure to meet these can have very serious consequences and is reported to the DCSF; failure in some detail or another has not been uncommon in independent schools.

Inspections have taken place once every six years, and that is the regularity you might still expect. They have extended into boarding and the early years. Under the third cycle (2010 onwards) inspections will be even shorter and lighter, but advance warning will be minimal: only five days or so. Regulatory issues will be essential and examined by one or two inspectors. If these are not met, a larger team will inspect a month later.

Failure will be reported to the department straight away. If a school is compliant, a short inspection is likely to follow in three years and another regulatory one in a further three years. Schools are able to commission a consultancy service to explore and report on any specific issues that may be of concern.

How will inspection affect a new member of staff? As a newly-arrived NQT, it might come in your first term or much later. You might not even experience it in your first job. Members of most staff rooms or common rooms view inspection with a degree of apprehension, but in a well-run school, senior managers should reassure you that such a process should be taken in everyone's stride. Good schools have nothing to fear; inspection inevitably raises some issues on which a school might improve.

You may well have one of your lessons observed. Most inspectors, if they have time, will offer a comment at the end of the lesson, but you will receive no detailed feedback. Inspectors may also observe you running an activity or society. You are less likely to receive any comment here, and indeed your visitor may well not stay for the entirety of the session. Don't infer anything from that. They have very busy schedules. You may well be asked by an inspector about the school induction process, or more probably about the induction process as an NQT. This latter is an obligation for them to explore.

You may, of course, find you are not overtly scrutinised at all. As the duration and nature of inspection has changed and shortened, more teachers find they are not observed. In many ways, it is the management of the school which is more under focus. You will, however, experience the sense of mild relief at the end. Some schools even stage a gentle celebration.

You are entering a very worthwhile profession. It is one which is enormously demanding of skill and emotional energy, but it is a rewarding one; one where your diverse skills may be employed; one where you may advance along academic or pastoral routes; one where, whilst term time may be exhausting, periods for recuperation exist. It is also, as this article has sought to explore, one in which the structures for induction, training, performance management and inspection are significantly better developed than they were when I began teaching. In short, checks are better balanced.

Chapter 14

Professional development issues within your first job

Paul Nials

If you are reading this chapter, I suspect that you are interested in the subject matter for one of two reasons. Either you will have completed your induction period recently and you are looking to make progress up the career ladder, or you are in a position to advise those who have just done so. Either way, there are no absolutes; no gems of erudite wisdom that are guaranteed to ensure success leading to rapid career advancement. However, there are some options open to you or those seeking guidance from you, and this chapter aims to explore some of the mechanisms and pathways that new entrants to the profession might reasonably consider.

So, as an enthusiastic new entrant to the teaching profession, what should you do next? In which direction should you seek to advance your career – academic, pastoral, extracurricular (or co-curricular)? Throughout your training and induction you will have been bombarded with opportunities to participate in a wide variety of activities both within and outside school. The key here is to be selective. Choose a pathway that will suit and interest you, be of benefit to the school and fulfil any obligations that you might have undertaken to your new employer.

Remember that you are bound by the commitments made in your letter of acceptance for your new job, so some further training may be necessary to help you discharge these responsibilities. This should be your first priority. However, in the furore to gain further qualifications and experience, it is important not to lose sight of the basics. It is necessary to sound a note of caution at this point.

Throughout this exploration of further training and continuous professional development, it is easy to overlook the central reason for being in school – namely, teaching. Most recently qualified teachers are still concerned from time to time about their own subject knowledge base. In the rush to seek career advancement, the everyday routine of planning interesting, effective, challenging and informative lessons can sometimes take second place. This, in my view, is a grave mistake. The most important critics of any teacher are the pupils. Your reputation in school as an effective teacher is founded on the quality of your performance in the classroom, so it is here that the consideration of professional development begins.

NQTs who have achieved QTS will have received a year of intensive training, the vast majority through the PGCE, if acquired recently at M level; otherwise through the Professional Graduate Certificate in Education or the GTP route. In addition, an induction period, typically of one year, will have followed on from this initial training.

The latter should also have included a carefully planned period of monitoring and target setting. Both these phases of training will have involved summative assessment against the Professional Teaching Standards. Initially, the assessment would have been made against the Qualifying or Q Standards, then in the latter stages of induction, against the Core or C Standards. Both these sets of standards require the trainee teacher or inductee to reflect on their practice and to be prepared to adapt it where benefits and improvements are identified (Standards Q7-8, C7-8). This demonstrates that they have developed into a reflective practitioner.

Of equal importance is the requirement to implement the improvements that were identified in the formative feedback given during training and induction: *ie* 'To act upon advice and feedback and be open to coaching and mentoring' (Standards Q9 and C9). These are fundamental cornerstones to improving professional practice and must be continued beyond the mandatory training period.

Without a constant reappraisal of teaching effectiveness, experiential learning is impossible. Brooks and Sikes[1] describe the reflective teaching cycle as 'Plan → Implement → Reflect → Evaluate → Plan' and so on. In well-run initial teacher training and induction programmes this cycle will be reviewed continually under the constructively critical gaze of the mentor or induction tutor.

I recall one of the more memorable quotes from my own MA(Ed) studies at the School of Education, University of Southampton, in 1997. I never managed to identify the source, but that fact doesn't detract from the significance of the content: 'Twenty years experience is not the same as one year's experience repeated 20 times.' In essence, without reflective practice, a teacher's skill set and appreciation of the complex process involved in teaching and learning will neither evolve, nor advance.

Whilst none of this is in any way revolutionary, it does raise the question: what happens after successful completion of the induction year? What mechanisms or processes are in place to ensure that reflective practices are encouraged or maintained? All too often the answer is: very few. However, all need not be lost and the continuation of basic practices can be very effective.

Few trainee teachers or NQTs will question the benefit of reflective practice. However, when the ink has dried on the final school stamp on the third induction assessment form, there will be other calls on the time of the now newly renamed Recently Qualified Teacher (RQT). The 10% timetable remission will disappear and other duties in school will beckon. This does not mean that the multitude of skills, such as evidence tracking, honed over the past two years need be relegated to the No Longer Used file. It is hoped that as an RQT, you will work in a school where Continuous Professional Development (CPD) is valued highly. Opportunities for In Service Training (INSET/D) may include attendance at examination board sponsored assessment and marking courses, courses aimed at developing pastoral skills or areas involved in curriculum development such as ICT.

The two core functions of these are the acquisition of knowledge about the process of effective teaching and gaining experience in a specific area, for example, assessment. In my opinion, attendance at such courses is essential and should be top of any need-to-do list. Providers of many of these one-day or short courses will often issue attendance certificates, which delegates duly file away with their notes from the day. While these

PROFESSIONAL DEVELOPMENT ISSUES WITHIN YOUR FIRST JOB

serve as a useful reminder to include the course on your CV, the reflective practitioner will note down the useful points that (s)he has gleaned and then make a series of action points stating how these will inform and improve their practice. Such jottings need not be exhaustive: it is the process of thoughtful integration which is important, not the paperwork generated.

Whilst on the topic of reflective practice, the process of lesson observation as an important mechanism for continued professional development needs to be highlighted. As a RQT you will be used to having an observer sitting at the back of your lessons, recording your progress. I hope that you would also be used to the constructively critical analysis of the lesson during the post-observation debriefing. This process of unpicking practice is central to effective reflection, but it need not end with the completion of induction.

Many schools now include teaching observation by peers as a requirement of their CPD policy. Such arrangements can lead to the evolution of true mentoring relationships in which both partners share equal status. Both benefit from the process. Even if it is not required specifically in your school, I would suggest that all RQTs seek such a relationship, preferably with a colleague who is more experienced, with whom they can work effectively, enjoy mutual trust and perhaps share some of the same teaching groups. I have found these pairings to be most effective when the participants teach in the same faculty, rather than in the same department.

Thus it is not always necessary to enrol on long externally-run courses in order to achieve professional development. Indeed, making best use of the opportunities available within one's own school can be a cost-effective way of enhancing professional performance. However, many such courses are available and many new entrants into the profession seek to continue their studies during their first job. One of the most obvious ways to do this is to build on the progress made during training. It has become increasingly common for higher educational institutions (HEIs) to offer Master's level studies during their PGCE courses. Currently, successful completion of the course at this level will reward the NQT with around a third of the 'credits' required to attain a Master's degree such as a MA(Ed). While this is great in principle, there are a number of points to note.

First, not all HEIs offering Master's degree courses will accept the credits from other universities. This is not a problem when an NQT has obtained a job in the same locality as the one in which they trained, but it can prove to be a real headache for those moving further afield – especially when the course requires regular attendance at the original university. Problems with transferability can mean that a potential applicant has to start from scratch all over again. One possible way around this is to contact the HEI of choice and see whether it is possible to submit the original work for consideration of remission against their assessment criteria.

Secondly, does the content of the course offered by a university fit your own CPD requirements? Master's degree courses vary greatly between HEIs but those offering modularity – where it is possible to select from a variety of courses to 'mix and match' according to your requirements – offer the greatest flexibility. By enrolling in a modular course it is possible to tailor the content to fit your own individual needs. This may include aspects of management, curriculum development (for instance in preparation for a head of department role), particular aspects of learning (SEN, SEAL) or more generic content such as mentoring and professional development of staff.

Finally, many of the Master's level courses require some form of dissertation. This can often be based on action research carried out in your own school. I have found this to be of great benefit if the subject for the investigation is chosen wisely. Like all aspects of effective CPD, it is essential to the senior management team of your school in any such decision.

However, if the government is successful (and this may prove to be a big 'if'), M level study for teachers is about to change with the introduction of the Master's in Teaching and Learning (MTL). The central idea is to make teaching more attractive as a career option by increasing its professional status. Another aim is to introduce greater structure into the first few years of teaching in order to raise standards.

First, unlike other forms of M level study for teachers, the MTL will be practice-based and the teaching will be split between a tutor from an HEI and a school-based 'coach'. It appears that the course structure will be modular, thus increasing flexibility and portability between schools. Ideally it would be a three-year programme that starts during initial teaching training and is completed in the year following induction. Current plans involve a variety of aspects of teaching including teaching and learning; assessment for learning; how children learn and develop; inclusion; curriculum and curriculum development; subject knowledge for teaching; leadership and management; and working with others in the children's workforce.

MTL will be rolled out in north-west England in summer 2010, when it will be offered to all NQTs. A national framework for the course has been developed by the Training and Development Agency for Schools (TDA) and is to be used by HEIs and schools as the basis for the degree programme. It is envisaged that in maintained schools, the in-school coaches will be trained through a centrally-developed national programme.

What is not clear at this stage is the effect that this will have on the independent sector. If the statements issued by the TDA stating that MTL will affect all teachers over the next ten years are correct, then the expectation will be that all members of the profession will have acquired a Master's degree. This sequence of events may have a profound impact on the CPD requirements of future NQTs. Watch this space!

There is no doubt that a formal qualification to acknowledge and reward achievement of your CPD is desirable. Furthermore, it reminds the newer entrants to teaching about what it is like to engage in the process of focused, formal study which is related closely to their work in the classroom. It also puts many of the theoretical concepts studied on PGCE/GTP courses into context.

However, the decision to undertake study at Master's level should not be taken lightly. Such courses, irrespective of their content and method of delivery, are costly both in terms of time and money. While the benefits to the individual can be considerable, it is essential that the SMT within the school is fully supportive of the process. Indeed, it may be necessary to request some time out of school to attend some aspects of the course. Heads will be mindful of the impact such training will have on their staff which in turn might detract from their primary role within the school – teaching. Anyone embarking on such a course must not only ask realistically what they hope to gain from such study but also what benefit will be gained by the school?

Some teachers have a very clear idea about their own career progression: their ultimate goal is Headship. If this is the case, further study, leading to enrolment on the National Professional Qualification for Headship (NPQH) course, may become the ultimate goal, although the qualification is not mandatory in the independent sector. This course is designed for experienced teachers who can provide evidence of expertise and experience across the six key areas of the National Standards for Headteachers.

After successful application, the trainee Headteacher will complete an online assessment profile and then attend an entry event over two days. As a result of this, a personalised programme, based on individual development needs, will be devised. This stage takes between four and 12 months, depending on the applicant's state of readiness for Headship. More information can be obtained from the National College for School Leadership (see URL at the end of the chapter).

If you are considering such a route, you will need to ensure that any additional training undertaken will count towards the evidence file required for application to the NPQH process. Several courses now state explicitly that they are suitable for this purpose. Of course, this is very much for the future: NQTs need to be sure that they are fully confident and competent in all the Core Standards before they consider additional training, especially training for Headship.

But what if you don't want to study for a Master's degree and the prospect of Headship is unappealing? My advice would be to look at the opportunities within your current school or sphere of interest and locate a gap in the market. Identify an area and create a niche that appeals to you. One good example is in the sphere of personal, social and health education (PSHE). This is a rapidly changing, and indeed expanding, area of educational provision. Yet it is sadly neglected by HEIs involved in teacher training and whilst much guidance has been issued by government, there are still far too few teachers willing to take on the role of coordinating this aspect the curriculum within schools.

However, good quality training is available, and if your school has established links with its Local Authority (LA), this training can be free of charge. The national PSHE CPD programme is run on behalf of the DCSF and Healthy Schools and is open to teachers who deliver, or contribute significantly to the delivery of PSHE in a school environment.

Training is normally delivered by a PSHE lead trainer within an LA, consists of around 30 hours of 'guided learning' and is supported by a range of online resources. It is also possible to complete the course via e-learning. Each course participant produces a portfolio of evidence which is formatively and then summatively assessed against the standards and programme criteria. This will also include observation of some lessons. If the submission is successful, it will lead to certification, and the course is accredited by one university for the purpose of further studies and will support teachers applying for other courses such as NPQH. Teachers in a number of independent schools have successfully completed this course, which they have found to be of great benefit to themselves and their employers.

For those wishing to assume some responsibility within school but who are less enthusiastic about further academic study, there are still a number of training avenues open. Many RQTs find themselves teaching in schools with a wide and varied extracurricular or co-curricular provision. For example, you may have played sport at university to quite a high level and now have an eye towards coaching school teams. My advice is simple. No matter what sport you have played, you will need to seek training in coaching and refereeing from an accredited body.

There is no doubt that being able to demonstrate a skill set within a sport is a great advantage. However, it does not automatically follow that you will be able to coach the sport effectively or, more importantly, safely. Furthermore, you will be dealing with pupils who are much less physically developed than you are, and so the drills and routines suitable for adults may not be suitable for them. Most of the major sporting bodies run accredited or certificated coaching, refereeing or umpiring courses. Once you have passed, these can be a valuable addition to any CV.

Most schools engage in some sort of outdoor pursuit activity or have a Duke of Edinburgh's Award (DoE) training programme. Once again, training is vital, not only for the safety of pupils in your care but for your protection as well. Mountain Leader Training UK provides a wide variety of courses which will enable school teachers to take groups of pupils into the hills safely. Alternatively, training to become a DoE leader opens another avenue for advancement.

As someone who spends a lot of time informing trainee teachers about the roles and responsibilities within teaching, I cannot emphasise enough how important it is to take all reasonable steps necessary to safeguard pupils in your charge. If you are considering any aspect of additional training for outdoor pursuits or sport, I would strongly suggest that you also seek a formal first aid qualification. In the unfortunate event of an accident, knowing what to do or more importantly what not to do is essential. St John Ambulance and the Red Cross run courses specifically for teachers and issue certificates of competence.

The suggestions contained within this chapter are by no means exhaustive and the area of continuing professional development is a rapidly changing one. However, I hope that I have given some insight into the variety of opportunities available to those seeking to advance during the all important first few years in their career.

Reference and Bibliography
1. Brooks, V., and Sikes, P. (1997): *The Good Mentor Guide, Initial Teacher Education in Secondary Schools*, Buckingham, Open University Press.

Useful websites:
www.mltuk.org
www.ncsl.org.uk
www.pshe-cpd.com
www.tda.gov.uk/teachers/mtl-aspx
www.teachingexpertise.com

Chapter 15

Looking ahead: the next steps

Tom Wheare

One of the inescapable features of teaching is the imposition of a complex timetable that gradually takes over your life, whose regularly sounded bells soon evoke Pavlovian responses! In all jobs there's a tendency to look forward to the weekend, but in teaching you can add the milestones of half terms and the holidays and a series of new beginnings which mark a path that, after a while, may begin to resemble a groundhog cycle.

Of course you will have experienced this as a student at school and university, but it feels – and is – different for teachers because, unlike their pupils, they are not on a comparatively rapid conveyor belt to the exit. On the contrary, a new academic year comes round and a new year group of pupils – and there you are still, essentially going through the same programme, like an eternal washing machine, even if the items in the drum change for each wash.

Fortunately, the infinite variety of the pupils, both in the classroom and in all the other activities of school, means that no two years are ever quite the same. And *you* change: you get better at your job; you develop new techniques; you teach different syllabuses and different year groups; you acquire QTS and, before long, responsibilities. The people round you change – you get to know them better, you welcome pupils and teachers newer to the school than you, and you gain an enhanced understanding of human nature, partly because you have seen something similar before.

But there will come a time when you think of making a more radical change and applying for a job elsewhere. Ideally you will be doing this at the right time and from a position of strength, not because you are unhappy with where you are and, above all, not because you feel you must bow to the received wisdom that you should move from your first school after two or three years.

Like all examples of received wisdom, this won't work for everyone and it's really only another milestone on the teacher's path – time, perhaps, to have a serious think about how you're getting on, a chat with someone you trust, a surreptitious peek at the *TES* – which is not, I can assure you, linked to an alarm on the Head's desk or covered with an invisible dye which will be revealed by the ultra-violet scanner issued as standard kit to all heads of department.

And it's perhaps worth adding that if you really think your present Head will react badly to the mere idea of your looking at another school, you may be working for a control freak from whom an early separation might be wise. Seeing what's out there is as likely as not to suggest that you are well placed where you are and, in any case, the bare advertisement won't tell you all you need to know about the kind of job it is or the kind of person they are looking for.

Time, then, to ask yourself what kind of person or future employee you are. What do you like or dislike about your present job? How well are you doing it and are you doing it better than you did at first? Which age group do you most like teaching and what do you most enjoy outside the classroom? Do you want to climb a ladder, and is this the right time to start? If so, which ladder is it to be – pastoral or academic – and is it planted in a day school or a boarding school? Are you happy with working in a co-ed environment or might you want to try teaching in a single-sex school?

Having got this far, there's quite a bit to be said for pausing and putting your initial conclusions into the context of your present school. After two or three years you will have worked out quite a bit about the school, including the internal promotions policy and the likely vacancies on the horizon. In nearly all schools, posts are advertised and, contrary to any rumours you may hear, not just stitched up before the vacancy is announced.

This is designed to allow people to declare an interest in the specific job and also, perhaps, to give an indication of their interest in promotion generally. It's not a bad way of giving the powers that be a nudge that you are reviewing the situation, but make sure you are ready to be taken seriously and that you have a genuine interest in the job. The process of being interviewed is nearly always valuable in itself and it is, of course, two-way. It's just as important that you should like them as that they should like you; that the job is the right one for you as that you are the right one for the job.

This can also, therefore, be a time for review. If you are to be the right person for the job, you need to know a reasonable amount about it, but you need to be very well aware of what you can offer, where your strengths and weaknesses lie, where you're coming from and where you think you're going. Your motivation is worth close examination. To what extent, if any, are you merely reacting to the things you have enjoyed so far, or to the things you really don't enjoy in your present job?

What about ambition? Teaching is a vocation and so it is, theoretically, perfectly possible to make it one's profession, as it were, and then remain a contented classroom teacher until you retire, never seeking promotion, simply and wholly fulfilled by practising your skill in the one area where it matters most, the classroom, and with the one group that is most important, the pupils.

It is, however, probably true that a teacher setting out to do this nowadays would raise doubts in the minds of colleagues and the Head. They might think it if not unnatural, then at least unorthodox, and circumstances might make it impossible. Teaching is both a profession in which, as Alice discovered through the looking glass, you have to run very fast just to keep up, but also one in which, if you stand still, you will not only fall behind, but you will become a stumbling block for others.

The pretty well inescapable requirement to move forward does not, however, mean you have to move on. There will be plenty of jobs to do and there will be posts of responsibility in your first school and it is as much the task of the senior management team and the Head to develop such opportunities for you as it is yours to seek them out. Career progression, therefore, does not necessarily mean a change of school.

Ploughing a long furrow usually means ploughing a deep one and there is a great deal to be said for schools having a number of long-serving staff. Experience enhances knowledge and gives perspective. On the other hand, there may be a lack of wider vision and a tendency towards conservatism, which is why most schools give at least serious consideration to external candidates for key posts such as house masters/mistresses and really quite often bring in outsiders to be deputy heads or heads of faculties such as science. Bearing that in mind, you may come to the conclusion that it is actually risky to stay in your first school and that a change may not just bring new opportunities; it may be the only way to guarantee a fulfilling career.

So let us assume you have thought it all through and come to the conclusion that it is time to look elsewhere and, indeed, found an advertisement in the *TES* or the ISC job zone that has caught your eye. In what way would you be a good candidate for the job? What strengths have you developed that would fit you for the post? How would you grade yourself against the person who holds a similar post in your present school?

You award yourself a good score on these initial tests and move on to consider the school advertising the post. What do you know about it and what can you find out, preferably from reliable and well-informed sources? Does it fit your base criteria – such matters as gender mix, academic standard, size, boarding or day, location and prospects? It is no longer a safe bet to assume that all schools are as safe as houses for the next ten years – or rather it is, but the state of the housing market is no longer synonymous with security.

And that market may very well play a part in determining your choice. Can you afford to live there and, if not, are you happy to be a commuter? Does the school offer accommodation and, if so, are the terms congenial? In boarding schools there is always a need for resident staff and the responsibilities that come with such posts can be very rewarding. On the other hand, this may be precisely the reason you are looking for a move, no longer enchanted by the proximity of young people, unable to lead the social life you would prefer or, put simply, about to set up with a partner and looking forward to developing a completely new life which has nothing to do with school.

Putting your domestic concerns to one side for the moment – but not forgetting them since they are of vital importance – what about the new school's reputation? Are you moving up-market academically and, if so, is your degree good enough to make you a runner? This may be the second and last time that your degree is a determining factor, but it is likely to be something the potential employer will look at. It is possible to overcome a poor degree, so don't rule yourself out if you are confident you have a lot to offer – and confident your referees will make it clear that your performance as a teacher more than compensates for the level of your qualifications on paper.

At my first interview all seemed to be going well when the Headmaster said: "One thing about you stands out a mile." I began to simper with modest expectation. "Your deplorable degree result!" Nevertheless, though thoroughly winded by this low blow, one which my high self-esteem had made completely unexpected, I was given the job – a one year stand-in for someone taking a sabbatical – and I stayed at the school for nine years.

This might be a good moment to consider whether some schools are better springboards than others, though if they are and if your mind runs along such lines, you would have needed to factor that in to your first job application to secure maximum uplift. It is probably true that some schools seem to provide a good many Heads and that others can honestly market their deputy headship with a strong likelihood of onward promotion within, say, five years.

Whilst the former does probably have something to do with the excellent and self-fulfilling reputation of a few leading schools, the latter is not an example of a network of power-brokers at work, but rather the fruit of a conscious policy. Schools which manage to deliver a fast track service via their deputy headship have made allowance for regular change at this level, choosing candidates who are aware of the likely outcome and keen to achieve it. Such schools will also have a need for longer-term leaders who provide the framework within which this policy can prove beneficial. None of this, however, should really be a concern two or three years into teaching and if it is, you may need to temper your ambition.

And are appointments made on the basis of who you know or how fruitful your present Head's grapevine is? No, because once people emerge from being applicants to being candidates, they have the same chance as everybody else. That's why being well prepared for your interview is important and why a genuine commitment to, and awareness of, the job you are being interviewed for is crucial. Technical or professional proficiency is important, but so is flair and breadth of awareness.

Heads are greedy people and they are always hoping to get something extra for nothing – what used to be called 'good schoolmasterly qualities'. If you are applying for a job that will involve managing colleagues, your personal qualities will be important and a wide-ranging contribution outside the classroom may suggest a willingness to look at things and people from more than one angle.

There are such things as shortage subjects and, statistically speaking, for what that's worth, a physicist or a mathematician may get shortlisted more frequently than equally talented colleagues who teach English or history. That could happen particularly when it comes to competition for posts of more general responsibility. A small school may well regard appointing a deputy head who can teach a shortage subject as a real deal-maker.

Even though it's probably too late for a classicist in their third year of teaching to retrain as a physicist, it's never too late or too early to engage in professional development. Such training is nearly always beneficial and it also conveys a message to your present school that you are not resting on your laurels. It provides an opportunity to talk to your head of department, and perhaps the person you work for within the school's pastoral structure, about the sort of development you are seeking.

This will lead, at the right time, to discussing your next career steps and one point on the agenda would quite properly be the question: should I stay here or should I have a look around? Remember, looking around and then applying is all you can do. It's up to other people whether you get asked to go for interview.

Applications are time consuming and presentation is important. Make sure that your side of things meshes accurately with their requirements. By doing so you will go some way towards deciding why you want the job and why you might be good at it. A good application form will give an instant impression of competence – and *vice versa*! You may be asked to make some of the application in handwriting and you may well be asked to provide a covering letter.

Both of these can be revealing – as can the ghosts of applications past. Spell-check, unfortunately, does not automatically replace the name of the previous school you really, really, really wanted to teach at with the name of the establishment you are currently courting! Be careful not to acquire the reputation of being a frivolous or flighty applicant. Beware that the independent sector is a relatively small world; Heads talk! It's not just your time that is consumed in this exercise, it's the time taken by potential interviewers and, much more importantly, the time you owe to your pupils when your mind and, indeed, body is elsewhere.

Transferring from the independent sector to the maintained one is the path less followed, but there are teachers for whom this might be the right step at the two- or three-year stage. It is probably true to say that the pedagogical structure is more evident in a maintained school. There genuinely are more hoops for the school, the teacher and the pupils to go through, but this is not necessarily a bad thing.

Personal success is perhaps easier to measure, and facing the challenges that bureaucracy adds to the already demanding job of teaching can stretch able minds and provide immensely worthwhile experience. The National Professional Qualification for Heads (NPQH) is not only mandatory for maintained sector Heads, but is a sensible target for teachers in both sectors; experience in the maintained sector would stand you in good stead if you decide to set off in pursuit of that qualification.

If at this point you are thinking that this chapter has at last got on to something relevant to you, the path to Headship, have a word with yourself! Do not wish your time away prematurely, and do not think that promotion is the most important objective. A young teacher has a unique opportunity to influence the minds and lives of students, simply by being young. A young teacher has a unique opportunity to learn from colleagues and to develop, both in human and professional terms. A young teacher has a unique opportunity to enjoy school life and life outside school; to relish the holidays; to flourish under the caring guidance of others; and to learn how to work well and how to enjoy doing so.

A great deal of emphasis is placed on teaching in the contemporary educational scene and far too much emphasis is placed on assessment. Learning is the key: your learning and, above all, your pupils' learning. If you can successfully impart what needs to be learned to those who need to learn it, who knows, your effect may be, like Dorothea's in *Middlemarch*, 'incalculably diffusive'.

Afterword

Nigel Richardson

When you are responsible for a book such as this, your text tends to arrive from contributors over an extended period of time. You edit it piecemeal, and only at the final stage do you get the opportunity to review it as a totality. For a variety of reasons, the period of time during which this collection of chapters took shape was longer than for the previous titles in the series, and the reviewing stage had to be brief – in order to meet the publisher's deadline – and the start of a new academic year, with its arriving cohort of NQTs.

As I read the text in its entirety from start to finish for the first time, I had only one real doubt about it: whether or not we had made it all look too daunting. If there is a common strand running through many of the chapters it is the variety and size of both the expectation and the demands made on teachers in the early stages of their careers: a package which includes the need to plan everything effectively; to take advice and occasionally to admit mistakes; to develop new skills; to deal sensitively yet firmly with people covering a wide span of ages, abilities, outlooks and ambitions.

That said, several contributors have stated in one way or another the immensely satisfying aspects of our work: its variety, the ability to work outdoors as well as indoors, in situations which involve not only formal teaching but also the sharing of hobbies and enthusiasms – and above all the thrill of helping to bring out latent talents; to steer young people towards new interests; to enable them to achieve things that they might never have believed possible for themselves; to play a part in moulding the lives of the next generation.

If you have persevered this far, my co-editor and I felt that you deserved a little light relief – in the form of the following spoof reference on a newly-qualified teacher. It first appeared in the *Times Educational Supplement* in June 1981 and was written by the late Ted Wragg, who was Professor of Education at Exeter University for many years. His regular column in the *TES*, about the imaginary local authority of Swineshire, poking fun at schools and those who worked in them, at educational jargon, bureaucrats and officialdom, and at many other aspects of school life, was a joy to a generation of hard-pressed teachers at that time, and we are very grateful to the editor of the *TES* for allowing us to reproduce it as our end-piece.

Referee's decision

Dear Elspeth,

Thank you for your letter bringing me up-to-date about your various job applications. I did indeed know that you have applied for 47 English posts, as I have written 47 references for you, though I did not know that you had had 14 interviews.

You say in your letter that you wonder if I am 'doing you down' in my references. God knows, Elspeth, I perjure myself enough in them to get Idi Amin [who was then dictator of Uganda – *Ed*] on the shortlist, but you must recognise that there is a limit.

It is most unfair of you to suggest that I do not stress the good work you did on your long teaching practice at North Swineshire Girls' Collegiate. You cannot, surely, have forgotten the fuss from parents about your project on Empathy. When I organised the National Association for the Teaching of English (NATE) workshop on 'Creative Writing Through Direct Experience' which you attended, I confess I never thought anyone would be so silly as to have pairs of pupils glue themselves together with Araldite, so that they could write about what it was like to be Siamese twins.

Also I warned you that Miss Ashcroft did expect a certain kind of formality in the school and that the girls were required to stand at the beginning of each lesson. Your regular opening 'Park your bums' was seen by the senior staff as somewhat deprecating of the school's traditions.

I know you tried hard to make up for these errors at the end of your teaching practice, but Miss Ashcroft has refused to wear the see-through blouse you bought her, nor did she appreciate your offering the school library copies of *Growing cannabis in a window box* and the cheap adolescent novelette *Boot in your groin*.

I have taken the liberty of ringing up one of two Heads of schools where you were called for interview, and I am sorry to hear that you did not really conduct yourself as sensibly as I should have hoped.

At West Swineshire Comprehensive, for example, the chairman of governors is not only extremely well-read, but is also president of the local English Language Society. He was most unhappy at an English teacher's use of crude Americanisms, and in any case it was tactless of you, at interview, to describe Milton as 'pure hogwash' and Shelley as 'so much horse manure'.

A Tyneside Headmaster told me you had rung up to ask if his school was in the North, as you had no intention of teaching people who talked like Scotsmen with their brains kicked in.

Strictly speaking, by the way, you should not be describing yourself to these Heads as having completed all the requirements of your PGCE. As you know, your long dissertation on sex education, consisting, as it did, of the single word 'Whoopee' typed over and over again on 43 sides of A4, was not up to the standard we require in this university, and you are deemed to have failed the theory part of the course until you resubmit a satisfactory piece of work. Incidentally, writing to the external examiner asking him to award you the NUT prize to help finance a boutique was without precedent in my experience.

I am glad you enclosed your next letter of application for me to cast an eye over, as presentation can matter when there are hundreds of applicants for posts. One or two little points do occur to me.

First of all, and this may sound a little old-fashioned, I think some Heads may look unkindly on the first page being lilac-scented notepaper, and the second lined Oxford pad paper with holes in the margin.

Another point which struck me was that you have written exactly the same letter as in your previous application to the Lake District school. Thus your offer to take fell walking and start a nature reserve may be thought unrealistic by the Head of Stepney, and you might give it further thought. He may also be a little put off by some of your spelling errors. I noted, among others, 'acuracy', 'exelence', 'standerds', and, when you were writing about how you felt at the end of teaching practice, 'nackered'. Perhaps you could, in any case, find a better choice of words here.

You ask about Miss Ashcroft acting as your referee instead of me, and I should not be offended at all by this, though I do remember her school practice report on you began 'If only her IQ was as high as her hemline' and went on to talk about your 'gauleiter approach to children'.

Finally I am sure that it is worth 'giving the independent sector a whirl' as you put it, but I should counsel against writing directly to Heads asking if any of their staff are 'about to croak'.

PS: In answer to your other query, of course you are free to apply for the vacant lectureship at the university, but since I shall be on the interviewing panel, would you mind using Miss Ashcroft as a referee?

If, in your first few years in teaching, despite all the positive experiences that our contributors have described, you are ever tempted to be discouraged or to apply for another job, just remember the Elspeths of the world, still aspiring to replace you.